SpringerBriefs in Energy

SpringerBriefs in Energy presents concise summaries of cutting-edge research and practical applications in all aspects of Energy. Featuring compact volumes of 50 to 125 pages, the series covers a range of content from professional to academic. Typical topics might include:

- A snapshot of a hot or emerging topic
- A contextual literature review
- A timely report of state-of-the art analytical techniques
- An in-depth case study
- A presentation of core concepts that students must understand in order to make independent contributions.

Briefs allow authors to present their ideas and readers to absorb them with minimal time investment.

Briefs will be published as part of Springer's eBook collection, with millions of users worldwide. In addition, Briefs will be available for individual print and electronic purchase. Briefs are characterized by fast, global electronic dissemination, standard publishing contracts, easy-to-use manuscript preparation and formatting guidelines, and expedited production schedules. We aim for publication 8–12 weeks after acceptance.

Both solicited and unsolicited manuscripts are considered for publication in this series. Briefs can also arise from the scale up of a planned chapter. Instead of simply contributing to an edited volume, the author gets an authored book with the space necessary to provide more data, fundamentals and background on the subject, methodology, future outlook, etc.

SpringerBriefs in Energy contains a distinct subseries focusing on Energy Analysis and edited by Charles Hall, State University of New York. Books for this subseries will emphasize quantitative accounting of energy use and availability, including the potential and limitations of new technologies in terms of energy returned on energy invested.

Wojciech Morawski · Adam Kałążny

The Taxation of Energy-Sector Assets: Polish Tax Legislation on the Eve of Energy Transformation

Springer

Wojciech Morawski
Department of Public Finance Law
Nicolaus Copernicus University
Toruń, Kujawsko-Pomorskie, Poland

Adam Kałążny
Poznań, Poland

ISSN 2191-5520 ISSN 2191-5539 (electronic)
SpringerBriefs in Energy
ISBN 978-3-031-15672-4 ISBN 978-3-031-15673-1 (eBook)
https://doi.org/10.1007/978-3-031-15673-1

This Springer imprint is published by the registered company Springer Nature Switzerland AG
The registered company address is: Gewerbestrasse 11, 6330 Cham, Switzerland

Preface

This study addresses an issue which is neglected in the context of the current energy transition processes that the European Union (EU), as well as Poland, is undergoing. The neglect of this topic is probably not due to economic irrelevance. Rather, it may stem from the incomparability of wealth taxation systems in different countries. Of course, wealth taxes are more 'separatist' than income or indirect taxes. In the case of the value-added tax (VAT), fairly uniform taxation rules apply throughout the EU. As a result, discourse among lawyers from different EU member states is quite easy. VAT lawyers must be familiar with EU regulations (and, thus, able to understand the regulations of other EU countries based on EU policies) because, without the knowledge of this and—above all—the jurisprudence of the CJ EU, they are unable to properly apply the goods and services tax per the Polish regulation (the Polish equivalent of VAT). In the case of income taxes, different countries' legal systems also share certain similarities. The very phenomenon of double taxation (and, as a result, the need to apply mechanism to avoid double taxation) requires mutual knowledge of legal solutions. Lawyers dealing with income taxation must at least generally understand other countries' legal constructs of income taxation if they work for taxpayers with international activities; otherwise, they will not help their clients. Also significant is the pursuit of income tax optimisation, which lawyers currently associate more with the phrase 'Base Erosion and Profit Shifting'.[1] If lawyers want to help clients apply tax optimisations,[2] they must be familiar with different countries' legal systems. In the case of income taxes, legal solutions may often not be uniform worldwide, but some typical solutions operate in individual countries.

Meanwhile, wealth taxes (paid on the possession or ownership of property) operate separately in each country. They are, to some extent, usually literally 'locked' within individual countries' borders. Conflicts between tax jurisdictions do not arise because, as a rule, tangible (in other words, *palpable*) property which is physically located in a given country is subject to taxation. Lawyers dealing with wealth taxation

[1] To learn more about the BEPS project, see https://www.oecd.org/tax/beps/.

[2] We leave aside the question of whether this optimisation does not already constitute tax avoidance.

in Poland may not be at all familiar with the regulations applicable in other countries. For practitioners, knowledge of other countries' wealth tax regimes is merely a matter of satisfying curiosity. Lawyer–practitioners do not need this knowledge to practise their profession.

This book's subject is the taxation of assets used for electricity generation (broadly defined). We deal with *energy* in the narrow sense as *electricity*. Raw materials, such as oil or gas (their extraction and transport), are dealt with only insofar as they serve to generate electricity. The book aims not only to describe the principles of wealth taxation but also to assess whether the regulation of wealth taxation in Poland affects the energy transition. Assessing whether the possible impact results from a conscious decision by legislature or is a side effect of existing legal solutions is also important.

Toruń, Poland Wojciech Morawski
Poznań, Poland Adam Kałążny

Contents

Chapter 1
Coal: Poland's Erstwhile 'Black Gold' or Current Problem?

Abstract Hard coal played a special role in Poland for many years. It (and lignite) was the basis for the entire power industry. It was not only economically important, but also emotionally important, which was partly justified historically. During the communist era, coal mining and metallurgy based on hard coal was the basis of an economy focused on the mass production of weapons. Currently, the Polish economy is undergoing a transition from a coal-based economy to a low-carbon economy. This is also a major social change. The old coal-bearing regions must find new ways of development for themselves.

Keywords Hard coal · Lignite · Coal-based economy · Low-carbon economy · Economic transition

Any discussion of the Polish energy sector must begin with coal, particularly hard coal. Poland's other energy resources are mainly imported products; coal alone is 'ours', and it has its own specific value, which is not only economic but also emotional. This book's authors learned as primary school children that hard coal is Polish 'black gold'. The roots of this specific relationship to hard coal should be sought in history. In the nineteenth century, coal-bearing regions were areas of economic development. Industry was concentrated in these regions, which were where people migrated. During the nineteenth century, in the areas that are currently Polish territory, hard coal was mined only in Upper Silesia (then part of Prussia) and the nearby regions of so-called Galicia (the part of Poland that had been occupied during the eighteenth century by Austria—the Cracow Coalfield) and the so-called Congress Kingdom (the part of Poland occupied by Russia—the Dąbrowa Coalfield) (Frużyński, 2012, p. 29). Coal mining in the area of Walbrzych in the Sudetes is less important since this region was not considered 'Polish' at the time.[1]

When Poland regained its independence in 1918, its incorporation of Upper Silesia was crucial to the state's functioning. At that time, the Polish territories that had been occupied for over 100 years by Russia and Austria were essentially agricultural and

[1] It was inhabited only by Germans, and Polish society was not aware that it had been part of the Kingdom of Poland in the Middle Ages.

W. Morawski and A. Kałążny, *The Taxation of Energy-Sector Assets: Polish Tax Legislation on the Eve of Energy Transformation*, SpringerBriefs in Energy,
https://doi.org/10.1007/978-3-031-15673-1_1

quite poor. Against this background, Upper Silesia stood out as one of the oases of affluence. It also had a well-developed industry and steel manufacturing—elements that were essential for the young state to build up its army.

The inhabitants of Upper Silesia, where coal was mined at the time, organised three uprisings (in 1919, 1920 and 1921) to become part of Poland. A miner was not just a miner. In Silesia, a miner was also an insurgent fighting to belong to Poland. From 1922 to 1939, Upper Silesia was widely autonomous (e.g. it had a separate budget) and differed in wealth from the rest of the country. In terms of earnings, miners were the elite in Poland at the time. Just before the outbreak of the Second World War, a worker in Poland earned—on average—140 zlotys, but a miner earned as much as 240 zlotys, or as much as a young army officer.[2]

During the period of communist rule, coal mining also occupied a special position since it was the basis for the development and operation of the heavy industry necessary for armaments. In a period of permanent crisis, which was an eminent feature of Poland's absurd communist economy, shops were in short supply of everything, and the communist authorities supported the miners in various way—a practice which was reflected in shops' much better provisions in mining regions. Moreover, for about 10 years (from 1970 to 1980), the leader of communist Poland was a miner—Edward Gierek—who also symbolised the mining industry's position. He cared very much for 'his' Upper Silesia and constantly emphasised that he had worked in mines (in Poland and Belgium) for many years. Nonetheless, Upper Silesia also joined the Solidarity movement.

The post-1989 period was a shock to the Polish economy, which was nevertheless crowned by dynamic development. The Polish economy was inefficient at the end of the country's communist period and, above all, energy-intensive. Electricity production was based on hard coal and lignite. The share of renewable energy sources was negligible (due, among other causes, to the fact that the only real option at that time was hydropower, the use of which is difficult due to the country's mainly flat topography).

With Poland's accession to the EU and subsequent economic policy of decarbonisation, tensions between Poland and the EU grew. The Polish economy was based on fossil fuels (especially hard coal and lignite, of which the EU disapproved) in a way not comparable to other EU countries.[3] As a result, Poland's transformation costs must be more burdensome for its economy. Decarbonisation was also a social problem since its negative social effects were concentrated in industrialised areas which, so far, have been engines of development and regions of above-average wealth.

For many years, the Polish authorities postponed difficult decisions, an approach which only exacerbated future problems. Of course, the energy transformation was

[2] https://nettg.pl/news/113976/na-co-bylo-stac-przedwojennego-gornika, retrieved: 30 June 2022.

[3] Note, however, that an examination of total CO_2 emissions does not present Poland as a particularly glaring example of a 'climate offender'. Between 2013 and 2020, Poland emitted 1,557,000,000 tonnes of CO_2, while Germany—whose population is just over twice the size of Poland's—emitted 3,395,000,000 tonnes. https://wysokienapiecie.pl/39431-co-polska-chce-ugrac-w-ue-przy-okazji-energetycznej-transformacji/.

taking place, but it was a slow process. As a result, in 2008, about 90% of Poland's electricity was still generated from hard coal (55%) and lignite (34%) (Kielerz et al., 2018, p. 88).[4] However, by 2020, coal's share of electricity production in Poland already amounted to 69.7%—that is, 3.9 p.p. less than the year before—while the renewable energy sources(RES 's) share had reached 17.7%. Gas's importance increased that year, with its share of the energy mix exceeding 10.1%, versus 8.8% in 2019. However, the significant reduction in coal use was largely due to the decline in energy demand as a result of the coronavirus disease 2019 (COVID-19) pandemic, the deteriorating competitiveness of domestic generation, cheap energy imports and increased generation from other sources.[5]

As we write this chapter, during the era of Fit for 55, acceptance of the realities of EU climate policy also prevails in Poland, and the dispute concerns only the pace of the transition away from hard coal and the degree of EU support for this process.[6] Interestingly, lignite does not arouse as many emotions as the liquidation of hard coal mining in Poland. Yes, in 2021, a dispute with the Czech Republic surrounded the Turów lignite mine,[7] whose closure was ordered by the EU Court of Justice.[8] However, this conflict was treated more as an instalment of the EU's long-standing conflict with the Polish government, rather than a dispute over energy.

Other fossil fuels also do not arouse much emotion in Poland in the context of shifting away from their use because they are essentially imported products.[9] From a political point of view, abandoning fossil fuels does not incur significant social costs, and it may also meet with social approval when fuels are imported from an aggressive Russia.

The COVID-19 pandemic has already significantly changed energy trends, supporting a shift away from coal. However, 2022 brought the Russian Federation's invasion of Ukraine. This aggression caused a sharp increase in the price of energy raw materials as a result of restrictions on their import from Russia. This problem lies not only in the price of these raw materials but also in their availability. As a result, coal has again become—at least from the perspective of a significant part of the country's population—the guarantor of Poland's independence. For the first

---

[4] Kielerz, A., Beuch, W., & Marzec, R. (2018). Węgiel w energetyce zawodowej a polski miks energetyczny. *Zeszyty Naukowe Instytutu Gospodarki Surowcami Mineralnymi i Energią Polskiej Akademii Nauk*, 105, 88. https://doi.org/10.24425/124380.

[5] https://www.forum-energii.eu/public/upload/articles/files/Raport_Transformacja%20energetyczna%20Polski_2021.pdf retrieved: 30 June 2022.

[6] https://wysokienapiecie.pl/39431-co-polska-chce-ugrac-w-ue-przy-okazji-energetycznej-transformacji/.

[7] The mine closure was impossible from the perspective of the Polish energy system and based on the operation of the surrounding towns, where flats were heated by the power plant at the mine.

[8] Order of the Vice-President of the Court of 21 May in Case C121/21-, Czech Republic v. Republic of Poland. ECLI: EU:C:2021:420.

[9] Poland imports about 70% of the gas it consumes and about 95% of its oil. Kielerz, A., Beuch, W., & Marzec, R., (2018). Węgiel w energetyce zawodowej a polski miks energetyczny, *Zeszyty Naukowe Instytutu Gospodarki Surowcami Mineralnymi i Energią Polskiej Akademii Nauk*, 105, 88. https://doi.org/10.24425/124380, retrieved: 30 June 2022.

time in many years, the Polish government is seeking to increase the country's coal output and not to close further mines. Climate problems are relegated to the background when the question of whether Poland will have sufficient power to generate electricity arises. Of course, awareness that a move away from coal must take place in the economy and, above all, in the energy sector is widespread, and the future is known to lie in renewable and low-emission energy. However, the mechanism for this process will change. No one in Poland wants to use gas as a source of energy during the transition away from coal. Coal reliance will probably persist longer than we thought just a few months ago, as Russia's ruler, Vladimir Putin, has decided.

Chapter 2
Real Estate Taxation in Poland: The Main Legal Problems

Abstract The regulation of real estate tax in Poland is characterised by both laconicism and vagueness. Regulations' content alone does not usually allow a legal problem to be solved—Polish administrative courts' jurisprudence must be referred to. Judgements of the Constitutional Tribunal are also important in these regulations' practical application. In particular, the judgement of the Constitutional Tribunal of 13 September 2011(P 33/09.) influenced the scope of the taxation of industrial facilities. Indeed, as a result of this judgement, these facilities' scope of taxation changed. It introduced formalistic criteria for determining whether a given facility is subject to the real estate tax, which is justified by the need to maintain constitutional standards.

Keywords Real estate tax · Agricultural tax · Forestry tax · Tax base · Tax rates · Land · Buildings · Structures

2.1 Introduction

In Poland, wealth taxes are usually understood broadly and divided into the following taxes:

a. the ownership or possession of property,
b. incremental wealth,
c. capital appreciation and
d. wealth transformation (Brzeziński, 2017, p. 178).

Taxes on wealth growth and asset appreciation are, to some extent, similar to income taxes. Classical income tax is usually paid when income is realised. Thus, a mere increase in the value of wealth does not necessarily generate an obligation to pay tax. Taxes under types b and c may be assumed to deal with a kind of 'hidden' income which has not yet been realised (i.e., usually, converted into money). Wealth transformation taxes are similar to turnover taxes, such as VAT and excise duty. For example, in Poland, there is a tax on civil law transactions, which—in simplified terms—is charged on the non-professional trade in goods, so it concerns (most often) private property and not property used for business activity. So, if someone sells their

W. Morawski and A. Kałążny, *The Taxation of Energy-Sector Assets: Polish Tax Legislation on the Eve of Energy Transformation*, SpringerBriefs in Energy,
https://doi.org/10.1007/978-3-031-15673-1_2

private car, the buyer will pay the tax on civil law transactions,[1] but if an entrepreneur (car dealer) sells new cars, the transaction will be subject to VAT.

Strictly speaking, wealth taxes are taxes on the ownership (possession or other forms of possession) of property. And this study focuses on these taxes. The wealth tax system (understood here as *taxes on the ownership of wealth*) comprises three main taxes:

- a real estate tax, regulated in articles 1a–7a of the Act of 12 January 1991 on local taxes and charges,[2]
- an agricultural tax, regulated by the Act of 15 November 1984 on agricultural tax,[3] and
- a forest tax, regulated by the Forest Tax Act of 30 October 2002.[4]

In a sense, these taxes should be treated jointly because they are quite similarly constructed (often, the same phrases are used in the acts creating them). Moreover, they complement each other. Indeed, they concern the same objects of taxation, though used for different purposes. These taxes concern both objects, which are *real estate* in the meaning of the civil law, and objects in some way permanent and connected with the land, even if—from the civil law point of view—they are not real estate.

They are distinguished from the tax on means of transport, which is regulated in articles 8 et seq. of the L.T.C.A. This tax is levied on trucks, buses, trailers and similar means of transport. Therefore, it is not very important from the perspective of electricity production, so it is omitted from this book. Similarly, the tax (formally called a *charge*) on dog ownership, which municipalities can introduce, is omitted.[5]

2.2 Real Estate Tax Terminology

The subjects of the real estate tax are:

- land (*grunty* in Polish),
- buildings (*budynki*) and
- structures (*budowle*).[6]

On the other hand, only land is subject to agricultural and forestry taxes. Land can only be subject to one of these three taxes.

The presentation of detailed solutions must be preceded by an explanation of the terminology used with respect to taxable objects other than land. The terminology

[1] Act of 9 September 2000 on tax on civil law transactions. Journal of Laws of 2022, item 111.

[2] Journal of Laws 2019, item 1170 as amended, hereinafter cited as the 'L.T.C.A'.

[3] Journal of Laws 2019, item 1256 as amended, hereinafter cited as the 'A.T.A'.

[4] Journal of Laws 2019, item 888 as amended, hereinafter cited as the 'F.T.A'.

[5] Article 18a, L.T.C.A.

[6] Article 2(1), L.T.C.A.

concerning real estate tax is based on the terminology used in the Act of 7 July 1994—Construction Law.[7] The terms used in this act are not at all clear, even to a person who uses Polish daily. Worse still, the act's terminology deviates greatly from everyday language. Sometimes two terms whose applications in the act are disconnected are treated almost as synonyms, even in dictionaries of the Polish language.[8] Therefore, this act created a specific terminology, the translation of which into a foreign language is very difficult—if possible at all. Therefore, the purposes of this book also require the creation of English terminology that will permit further considerations.

In Polish law, the broadest category is an '*obiekt budowlany*', which we translate as a 'construction object'. This term includes: '*budynek*' (in English, a building), '*budowla*' (a structure) and '*obiekt małej architektury*' (a small architectural object), including installations that ensure that an object can be used in accordance with its purpose and erected using construction products.[9]

The term 'building' is defined in the Local Taxes and Charges Act as a construction object within the meaning of the construction law, which is permanently connected to the ground, separated from the space by means of building partitions and has foundations and a roof.[10] Meanwhile, a 'structure' is defined as a construction object within the meaning of the construction law, which is not a building or a small architectural object, as well as a construction device within the meaning of the construction law connected to a construction object, which ensures that the object can be used for its intended purpose.[11] The above-mentioned construction device is defined by the construction law as technical equipment connected with a construction object, ensuring the possibility to use the object for its intended purpose, such as connections and installation devices, including those used for treating or collecting sewage, as well as passages, fences, parking places and places for rubbish bins.[12]

A 'small architecture object' is defined only in the construction law. In accordance with this act, such an object should be understood as small objects, particularly:

a. objects for religious worship, such as shrines, wayside crosses and statues,
b. statues, water features and other garden architecture objects,
c. utility objects for daily recreation and the maintenance of order, such as sandpits, swings, ladders and bins.[13]

---

[7] Journal of Laws of 2019, item 1186, hereinafter referred to as the 'construction law' or 'C.L.A'.

[8] For average Poles, the distinction between the Polish terms 'budowla' and 'budynek' is most often completely incomprehensible. They understand the terms to mean something results from construction activity, something built, and they will almost certainly (unless they are specialists in construction law) not be able to explain the difference between the two terms. However, against the background of the construction law and, consequently, the Act on Local Taxes and Charges, this distinction is crucial.

[9] Article 3(1), C.L.A.

[10] Article 1a(1)(1), L.T.C.A.

[11] Article 1a(1)(2), L.T.C.A.

[12] Article 4(9), C.L.A.

[13] Article 3(4), C.L.A.

Note, however, that in the construction law, the terms 'structure' and 'building' both have their own definitions, which differ slightly from those in the Local Tax and Charges Act, unfortunately leading to additional confusion. These concepts will be analysed in detail below.

2.3 Real Estate Tax on Buildings

2.3.1 The Concept of Buildings

The definition of a 'building' quoted above (Sect. 2.2. *Real Estate Tax Terminology*) causes much controversy in practice. For example, judicial decisions are inconsistent as to whether a building that has only part of its roof is still a taxable building. This ambiguity is part of the wider problem of taxing buildings that are no longer in use for some reason. This problem does not necessarily just concern buildings that are part of abandoned industrial facilities; it also concerns buildings that are not in use while, at the same time, other elements of an entire industrial complex are still used to carry out economic activities. In the jurisprudence of Polish courts, an opinion has formed that the roof's technical condition (or other elements of the building) or completeness does not affect whether the object is a building within the meaning of the Act on Local Taxes and Charges and, consequently, whether it is subject to taxation. The roof's condition, damage or removal of a significant part does not mean that a given object lacks a roof and, therefore, ceases to be a building within the meaning of the tax act. Only an object which is completely and permanently deprived of a roof ceases to be a building within the meaning of the tax law, or even a construction object within the meaning of the provisions of the construction law.[14] More general views are formulated here that an object remains a building in tax terms even when—for technical, legal or factual reasons—it is not and cannot be used.[15] Such an approach is justified by the purpose of real estate tax as a tax related to the very act of owning property and not to the act of obtaining income with the property's help. A separate problem is the amount of the tax. In this context, the non-use of the object may influence the tax burden.

A much more serious practical problem is whether the concept of a *building* should also include the technical equipment installed in buildings, or whether such equipment should be treated as separate objects. Acceptance of the latter concept allows for taxing these devices (or at least their constructional portions, such as foundations) as structures. We discuss these issues when analysing the taxation of

[14] See, e.g., the following judgements of the Supreme Administrative Court: of 28 March 2018, II FSK 762/16, of 19 January 2017, II FSK 2381/16, of 14 November 2014, II FSK 2680/12, of 3 April 2014, II FSK 812/12, of 29 November 2013, II FSK 2944/14 and of 20 December 2012, II FSK 715/11.

[15] Judgement of the Supreme Administrative Court of 29 November 2018, II FSK 1605/18.

particular types of energy-related facilities (Chap. 5. *The Taxation of Construction Objects Used to Generate Energy: The Current Legal Regime*).

2.3.2 The Tax Base

The taxable base for buildings in Poland is their usable area (Article 4[1][1], L.T.C.A.), which is measured along the internal length of the walls on all floors, with the exception of staircases and lift shafts. The following are also considered 'storeys': underground garages, cellars, basements and attics (L.T.C.A., Article 1a[1][1] and Article 1a[1][5]). Therefore, in practice, any space in a building can be considered a storey, even if it is not a storey based on the provisions of the construction law. However, this consideration does not mean every storey will be taxable. The areas of the rooms or portions thereof and the part of the storey with a height between 1.40 m and 2.20 m are included in the usable area of the building only as 50% of the actual area, and if the height is less than 1.40 m, this area is omitted.[16]

In the practical case of industrial facilities, which have a much more complicated structure than typical residential buildings, determining whether a given horizontal plane is already a storey can sometimes be very difficult. The solution to this difficulty may be the principle of resolving doubts in the taxpayer's favour, which is well established in Polish tax law.[17] It applies both to doubts that cannot be resolved regarding the interpretation of a provision of tax law[18] and doubts related to the determination of the case's facts.[19]

2.3.3 Tax Rates

Tax rates apply to buildings depending on their purpose and nature. They may vary from municipality to municipality since the tax law only sets maximum limits for each type of building.[20] Within a municipality, rates are set by the municipal council.

The highest maximum rates apply to buildings or portions thereof connected to business activity and residential buildings or portions thereof occupied for business activity—25.74 PLN (*polski złoty*)[21] per 1 m^2 of usable area. The lowest rates apply

---

[16] Article 4(2)(2), L.T.C.A.

[17] The Latin phrase 'in dubio pro tributario' is usually used in Poland. For more on this principle, see, inter alia: Mariański, A. (2011). Janicki, A. (2021).

[18] This solution is explicitly formulated in Article 2a of the Tax Ordinance Act of 29 August 1997, Journal of Laws of 2021, item 1540, as amended.

[19] This aspect is not formulated explicitly in a specific legal provision but derived from the entirety of tax law regulations and constitutional principles.

[20] Article 5 L.T.C.A.

[21] On 30 June 2022, the exchange rate of EUR 1 was PLN 4.68.

to residential buildings or portions thereof –0.89 PLN per 1 m^2 of usable area.[22] Other buildings or portions thereof may be taxed at the maximum rate of 8.68 PLN per 1 m^2 of usable area.[23]

Therefore, although buildings' tax base in no way relates to their value, tax rates are related to buildings' potential capacity to generate revenue. However, this relationship is very loose.

2.4 The Real Estate Tax on Structures

2.4.1 The Concept of Structures

The taxation of structures is one of the most controversial issues in Polish tax law. This problem lies in the understanding of the term 'structure'. Paradoxically, although the term's definition presented above is in use, in practice, it does not much help taxpayers—first because it is logically flawed and, second, because, as a result of the definition's defects, the Constitutional Tribunal and the administrative courts have elected to develop a 'quasi-definition' of the term. Unfortunately, administrative courts' jurisprudence can hardly be assessed as consistent. Rather, it constitutes a long-standing search for a solution to this problem, which is increasingly detached from the content of the provisions of the Act on Local Taxes and Charges. Surprisingly, this one concept can be the subject of so many contradictory rulings. (Morawski, 2012, pp. 51–257).

The essence of the problem of concept of structure lies in the fact that tax regulations, in defining the concept of a structure as a taxable object, refer to the construction law. Pursuant to Article 1a(1)(2) of the L.T.C.A., a 'structure' comprises the following objects:

1. a construction object within the meaning of the construction law which is not a building or a small architectural object and
2. a construction device within the meaning of the construction law—in this case, linked to a construction object—which ensures that the construction object can be used for its intended purpose.

The most serious problems relate to the first part of the definition, which concerns a construction object within the meaning of Article 3(1) of the C.L.A. The definition of a 'construction object' was amended on 28 June 2015; this amendment, however, did not solve the problem of the definition being logically flawed. Until 28 June 2015, it read as follows:

---

[22] The rates applicable in 2022, which are valorised annually, are provided. On 3 January 2022, the Euro (EUR) exchange rate was PLN 4.5889.

[23] Rates for specific building categories, such as those related to medical treatment or the manufacture of certain agricultural products, have been omitted.

1. A construction object shall be construed as:
   a. the building, including technical installations and equipment;
   b. a structure which forms a whole from the technical and functional point of view together with its installations and equipment;
   c. small architecture object.

The definition, thus, referred to the definition of a 'structure' in Article 3(2) of the C.L.A. The definition of a 'structure' in the C.L.A. comprises two parts. The first part is 'any construction object which is not a building or a small architectural object'. Meanwhile, the second part contains an illustrative enumeration of structures presented as examples: 'airports, roads, railway lines, bridges, flyovers, tunnels, technical networks, freestanding aerial masts, freestanding advertising devices permanently connected with the ground, earth, defence (fortification), protective, hydrotechnical structures, tanks, freestanding industrial installations or technical equipment, sewage treatment plants, waste dumps, water treatment stations retaining structures, above-ground and underground passages for pedestrians, land development networks, sports structures, cemeteries, monuments, as well as construction parts of technical equipment (boilers, industrial furnaces and other equipment) and foundations for machines and equipment, as technically separate portions of objects constituting a functional whole'.[24] Notably, this definition is similar to the definition of a 'structure' in the L.T.C.A., but it differs in that it contains an example (at least when relying on the linguistic interpretation of the legal regulation) of objects that are structures.

This definition clearly defies logic. The definition of a 'construction object' refers to the definition of a 'structure', and vice versa. This interdependence creates a vicious circle of reference. In a judgement of 13 September 2011,[25] the Constitutional Tribunal held that this provision—despite its illogic—is consistent with the Polish Constitution, albeit under certain conditions. Interestingly, the Constitutional Tribunal was fully aware that the regulation was flawed, which it unequivocally demonstrated and strongly criticised in justifying the judgement. However, the tribunal decided that, with the acceptance of certain conditions (which, in practice, will limit the scope of real estate taxation), the regulations may still apply.

First, in the opinion of the Constitutional Tribunal, only those structures that are defined 'by name' as structures in the construction law may be taxed. Such an indication of a given object as a 'structure' need not be provided for in the definition of a 'structure' itself, but it may also be provided for in other provisions of the construction law. Thus, a very formalistic criterion was formulated which determines the scope of taxation. The tribunal justified its standpoint by the fact that tax regulations must be

---

[24] We quote here the original wording of the catalogue of structures contained in Article 3(3) of the C.L.A., which was later subjected to numerous changes. These changes will be analysed further since they influenced the practice of taxing energy facilities (Chap. 3. The Taxation of Assets Used to Extract Energy Resources).

[25] P 33/09.

precise and that only structures which unquestionably fall within the scope of taxation may be subject to taxation. No doubts as to the disadvantages facing the taxpayer may be resolved here, for example by reasoning per analogiam. The Constitutional Tribunal once again confirmed the validity of the in dubio pro tributario principle in Polish tax law (which suggests that doubts concerning the interpretation of tax law should be resolved in the taxpayer's favour). This ruling meant that the determination of whether a given object were subject to real estate tax was based on finding the name of the given type of object in the construction law. Given the ambiguity of many of the terms used in Article 3(3) of the C.L.A. and constant technical developments, which involve the emergence of new types of construction objects, this task is often very difficult.

A separate area of dispute is whether a given object is taxable as a whole or whether only its construction parts should be taxed. The first view has usually been presented by tax authorities, relying in this case on the definition of a 'structure' in which (until 28 June 2015) the following phrase appeared: 'a structure constituting a whole in technical and functional terms, together with installations and equipment'. In turn, taxpayers referred to a fragment of the definition of a 'structure'—'as well as the building portions of technical equipment (boilers, industrial furnaces, wind power plants, nuclear power plants and other installations) and foundations for machinery and equipment'—to demonstrate that only the construction part of the structure was taxable. Unfortunately, the administrative courts have inconsistently resolved this dispute. A detailed description of the administrative courts' jurisprudence concerning particular types of structures will be presented in the following chapters (Chap. 3. The Taxation of Assets Used to Extract Energy Resources; Chap. 5. The Taxation of Construction Objects Used to Generate Energy: The Current Legal Regime). We must observe, however, that the administrative courts have not developed a coherent approach in this regard. For one type of industrial facility, the prevailing view is that only their construction parts are taxable (see Chap. 5: 'Taxation of Onshore Architectural Objects Used to Generate Energy: The Current Legal Regime'). For other types, whole facilities are taxable (e.g. LNG regasification stations[26]), and for still others (electrofilters and transformers), the jurisprudence varies (see Chap. 10: 'Electric Transmission Lines and Equipment: The History of Unexpected Legal Changes and the Courts' Unstable Approach').

Even the statement that only the construction part of a facility is taxable does not mean that the taxation of the entrepreneur's assets can be established, due to practical problems related to the determination of the 'boundaries' of the construction part. The next stage is to determine the value of this portion, which also gives rise to disputes in practice.

Since 28 June 2015, the definition of a 'structure' has changed. Notably, this change happened somewhat accidentally since, when amending the C.L.A., members of Parliament did not initially realise that they could change the scope of real estate taxation (Morawski, 2015, pp. 23–31). Since then, the definition of a 'construction object' has been as follows: a building, a structure or a small architectural object,

[26] Judgement of the Supreme Administrative Court of 13 May 2014, II FSK 1360/12.

together with installations ensuring that the object can be used in accordance with its intended purpose, erected using construction products. A vicious circle of references is still implied (as a result, the Constitutional Tribunal's judgement cited above (Sect. 2.4.1. The Concept of Structures) remains valid), but fragments indicating a structure as a whole from the technical and utilitarian point of view are no longer included. Thus, this new definition supports the (unintentionally) slow evolution of the jurisprudence towards the view that only the construction parts of technical equipment are subject to the real estate tax.[27]

In practically applying real estate tax regulations, finding an appropriate name in the list of objects which are structures is crucial, and this list is included in Article 3(3) of the C.L.A. Obviously, the names of a considerable amount of objects which are connected to the power industry are not included in this list. However, they can be included in a more general category: 'construction parts of technical equipment'. In this case, however, only their construction part is subject to taxation. This solution is advantageous for the taxpayer, which is why it is usually aimed at convincing the court that a given object falls into this category of structures.

In the original version of the C.L.A., the relevant enumeration in Article 3(3) (already quoted above, Sect. 2.4.1. The Concept of Structures) included, inter alia, the following passage: 'as well as the construction parts of technical equipment (boilers, industrial furnaces and other equipment) and the foundations of machinery and equipment, as technically distinct parts of objects constituting a functional whole'. The enumeration in parentheses was insignificant since the provision referred to any technical equipment and its construction parts. Interestingly in practice, however, as of 29 September 2005, the addition to the enumeration (after the words 'industrial furnaces') of the phrase 'wind power stations' has resulted in a change to the administrative courts' line of decisions. These courts have held that only the building portion of a wind power plant is taxable since that date.[28]

In this way, a rather strange method (from the perspective of the principles of legal text interpretation) of resolving doubts about the taxation of industrial facilities (especially those related to the power industry) was formed. The legislator simply added (or subtracted) some names from the enumeration: 'construction parts of technical equipment (boilers, industrial furnaces and other equipment)'. Other changes were also made to the catalogue of structures. These changes are worth presenting for the purpose of further analysis.

Thus, since 17 July 2010, a 'linear object' has appeared, defined in Article 3(3a) of the C.L.A. as 'a construction object, the characteristic parameter of which is length, in particular a road with an exit, a railway line, a water pipeline, a canal, a gas pipeline, a heat pipeline, a pipeline, an electrical power line and traction, an overhead cable line and an underground cable line placed directly in the ground, a floodbank and a cable duct, whereas cables installed in it do not constitute a construction object or

---

[27] However, this view does not mean that the jurisprudence is fully uniform. See the judgement of the Supreme Administrative Court of 22 July 2020, II FSK 1064/20.

[28] See, e.g., the judgement of the Provincial Administrative Court in Szczecin of 23 February 2011., I SA/Sz 887/10.

a part thereof or construction device'. Since 1 July 2011 (related to plans to build nuclear power plants), an addition was also made to the phrase 'construction parts (of boilers, industrial furnaces and other equipment)': 'nuclear power plants'. This addition protects the investor from the risk of a gigantic tax burden calculated on the value of, among other things, a reactor. In turn, on 16 July 2016, wind power plants were removed from the calculation, but they were reinstated on 1 January 2018 (see Chap. 6: 'The Taxation of Wind Power Plants: A Case of Regulatory Instability'). On 18 February 2021, offshore wind turbines were added, and this addition was again related to the planning of major investments in this area. Clearly, legislators want to protect costly energy investments from the risk of excessive tax burdens. (This protection does not apply only to completely ill-considered changes concerning wind power plants.)

2.4.2 *Taxable Structures*

Notably, only those structures which are 'connected with the conduct of business activity' are subject to taxation. This concept is defined in Article 1a(1)(3) of the L.T.C.A., according to which structures connected to the pursuit of business activity should be understood as structures owned by an entrepreneur or other entity who is conducting business activity (with certain exceptions). 'Business activity' is understood here as an organised, profit-making activity conducted continuously on one's own behalf. However, 'business activity' does not include farming and forestry activities, nor—for example—letting rooms to tourists on agro-tourism farms (under certain conditions).[29]

The concept of a business connection and, particularly, the distinction between a business connection and a business occupation are analysed in further detail in Chap. 7: 'The Taxation of Land Related to Energy Production'.

2.4.3 *The Tax Base*

The tax base depends on whether a property is depreciable for income tax purposes.

In the case of depreciable objects, this value forms the basis for the calculation of depreciation charges in a given tax year (the so-called initial value determined, in principle, at the time when the object starts to be used in the course of business).[30] In practice, this value is determined when the object is put into use or acquired. It is, therefore, a historical value that is not related to the current market value of the structure in a given year. Structures that have already fully depreciated are still taxed on the basis of their value for depreciation purposes, except that the value on

[29] Article 1a(1)(4), L.T.C.A.; Article 3, Entrepreneurs' Law Act (2021, item 162).

[30] Article 4(1)(3), L.T.C.A.

1 January of the last year in which a depreciation write-off was made is used, and it is not reduced by depreciation write-offs.[31] This value is the initial value determined for depreciation purposes, sometimes many years before.

For non-depreciable (and previously not depreciable for a taxpayer) structures, the taxable base is the structure's market value as of the date when the tax obligation arose—that is, the year when the structure was acquired or constructed by the taxpayer. Again, this value is the structure's historical value, and it does not refer to the structure's real value during the year of taxation. In a sense, structures in Polish real estate tax are always treated as new structures since their tax value is calculated as if they were new.

Inflation mitigates, to some extent, the effects of linking the tax base to a structure's historical value. However, the lack of inflation means that the actual tax rate in relation to the structure's market value in a given tax year is actually higher than the statutory 2%. This problem is particularly significant if the technical portions (and not only the construction parts) of technical equipment are also subject to taxation. This particular significance is due to the equipment's value decreasing over time, owing not only to wear and tear but also to technical progress.

The lack of an object's depreciation can usually be due to the lump-sum method of income taxation when no income has to be determined. This situation is increasingly common in Poland. However, a taxpayer may also generally depreciate objects but be unable to depreciate a particular object because, for example, they do not currently use the object for business purposes. Quite often, however, an entire object is depreciable (constituting one so-called depreciable fixed asset) but only its construction part (usually the equipment's foundation) is taxed. In this case, the value that forms the basis for calculating the depreciation of the object's construction part cannot be identified. As a result, the value of the tax base must be determined as per structures that have not depreciated.[32]

Disputes over the understanding of the concept of a 'structure' (and inconsistent jurisprudence), as well as the manner in which the tax base is constructed, mean that the tax burden amount is largely a matter of chance. As a result, comparing the tax burden of different types of energy facilities in Poland is difficult. Apart from different courts' potentially different rulings on what is—in fact—taxable, the key difficulty in this regard is the point at which the amount that makes up the tax base is determined. Not uncommonly, two identical structures are charged different real estate tax amounts because they were built in different years. It must be remembered that, in the 1990s, Poland faced high inflation.[33] As a result, older objects are taxed at much lower rates despite the fact that, sometimes due to conservation, they still retain their market value and efficiency. Additionally, determining the historical market value of complex objects' construction parts is very complicated. The observation

---

[31] Judgement of the Supreme Administrative Court of 3 March 2021, III FSK 999/21.

[32] Judgement of the Supreme Administrative Court of 10 January 2020, II FSK 3818/18.

[33] Poland's inflation was as high as several hundred per cent per annum, falling only to less than 50% per annum in 1992 before dropping to less than 20% in 1996. See https://300gospodarka.pl/news/inflacja-w-polsce-na-przestrzeni-lat-wykresy-gus, retrieved: 30 June 2022.

of valuers' practices leads to a rather sad conclusion about valuations' correctness and valuers' understanding of what is expected of them.

By its nature, the value determined for depreciation purposes (the so-called initial value) does not always correspond to a structure's market value because the initial value is determined for a specific purpose: to determine the point at which investment costs are deducted in order to calculate income tax. For example, Polish legislators decided that, as a rule, interest on a loan drawn to construct a fixed asset (a structure) incurred up to the moment of putting the asset into use is included in the structure's initial value. Therefore, they are deducted only together with the depreciation write-offs. On the other hand, interest incurred thereafter is deducted at the time it is incurred. As a result, the method of financing (in the case of financing from the taxpayer's own funds, the initial value of the object will be lower, than if the investment is financed through a loan) and the moment of taking the loan (the earlier it is, the more interest will be included in the initial value) affect the determination of the tax base. Therefore, not uncommonly, the owners of two identical structures have to pay different amounts real estate tax amounts.

2.4.4 *Tax Rates*

The maximum real estate tax rate on structures is 2% of the tax base.[34] A municipal council may set this rate and vary it, in principle, freely—as long as it does not infringe upon constitutional standards (e.g., the principle of equality). In practice (due to municipalities' difficult budgetary situation), the application of a rate lower than the maximum rate is very rare.

2.5 A Building or a Structure? Unclear Boundaries

The distinction between 'buildings' and 'structures' is problematic for several reasons. Essentially, a 'building' is an object that includes an area separated by building partitions and that forms the basis for taxation. Problematically, however, this fragment of the object which is separated by building partitions (which need not be classical walls) is very often small in relation to the whole object. This case increases the risk of a dispute with the tax authority, which will claim that the dominant features of a given object are the features of a structure.

An administrative court's judgement is always uncertain in this case because the courts increasingly often opine that an object which meets all the conditions contained in the definition of a 'building' will not always be a building. From the perspective of this book's subject, the most important view expressed in the jurisprudence holds

[34] Article 5(3), L.T.C.A.

that objects which meet the conditions for being regarded as 'buildings' will nevertheless not be buildings but, rather, structures if their 'name' is included in the list of structures[35] or if their 'distinguishing feature' is not their usable area.[36]

This book's authors disagree with the jurisprudential concepts presented above. A comparison of the definitions of a 'structure' and a 'building' clarifies that structures can only be objects that are not buildings. If an object could potentially qualify as both a building and a structure, it should be taxed as a building.

2.6 The Taxation of Land with the Real Estate, Agricultural or Forestry Tax

2.6.1 The Demarcation of the Real Estate Tax, Agricultural Tax and Forestry Tax

Land may be subject to the real estate tax, forestry tax or agricultural tax. As we have already indicated, these taxes do not differ significantly in terms of their legal construction. However, they exhibit significant differences in tax rates and the cataloguing of tax reliefs and exemptions. As a rule, the agricultural and forestry tax rates are significantly lower than the real estate tax rates. This difference can be justified by the fact that agricultural and forestry taxes concern a relatively low-profit sphere of economic activity.

Due to significant differences in tax burdens, deciding when land should be subject to the real estate tax and when it should be subject to the agricultural or forestry tax is crucial. Legal regulations have adopted the principle that all land is subject to the real estate tax unless it falls under categories that are subject to the agricultural or forestry tax.

In principle, forests or agricultural land should be subject to the forest tax or the agricultural tax, respectively. The peculiarity of the Polish system of land taxation is that the way land is used does not determine taxation; rather, taxation is determined based on the land and buildings register maintained by local government units (poviats or municipalities),[37] and this approach follows from the executive regulation of the Geodetic and Cartographic Law.[38] Sometimes in practice, even in city centres, land is formally defined in the land and building register as 'agricultural land'.

This does not mean that land used for industrial purposes and wrongly classified as 'agricultural' will always be subject to the agricultural tax. The tax authority may

[35] Judgement of the Supreme Administrative Court of 8 May 2018, II FSK 1281/16.

[36] Resolution of the Supreme Administrative Court of 29 September 2021, III FPS 1/21.

[37] According to Article 1a, paragraph 3 of the L.T.C.A., 'By the terms used in the Act: (1) agricultural land, (2) forests, (3) wasteland […]—means land classified as such in the land and buildings register'.

[38] Act of 17 May 1989, Geodesic and Cartographic Law (Journal of Laws of 2020, No. 276, as amended).

tax this land with higher real estate tax rates; however, it must prove that the land was occupied for the purpose of conducting business activity. Agricultural land and forests are always subject to the real estate tax if they are occupied for business activity.[39] However, only the portion of the land on which such an activity is conducted (and not the entire registered plot of land) will be occupied to carry out business activities.

2.7 The Tax Base

For the real estate tax and forestry tax, land is taxed on the basis of its area. This area is determined from the land register.

In the case of the agricultural tax, the area is the taxable base only if the land does not exceed one hectare. If a taxpayer owns land that covers a larger area, the so-called number of conversion hectares must be calculated. This calculation involves applying conversion factors to the actual land area in order to determine its potential usefulness for agricultural production.[40]

2.7.1 Tax Rates

The maximum (selected) real estate tax rates for 2022 are as follows:

- on land connected with business activities, irrespective of the qualification in the land and building register, PLN 1.03 per 1 m^2 area,
- on underlying or flowing surface waters of lakes and artificial reservoirs, PLN 5.17 per 1 ha of area, and
- on other land, including land occupied for the conduct of paid statutory public benefit activity by public benefit organisations, PLN 0.54 per 1 m^2 area.

2.8 Business Connections and Occupations

Two phrases have repeatedly appeared in the above discussion: (1) land or building occupied for the conduct of a business and (2) land, a building or a structure connected to the conduct of a business.

The legislation does not define ‘occupied for business purposes’. In practice, it is assumed that this phrase refers to a situation in which activities that constitute economic activity are actually performed on the land or in a building or structure.

[39] Article 2(2), L.T.C.A.

[40] Article 4, A.T.A.

The term 'land, buildings and structures connected to business activities' is defined in the L.T.C.A.[41] According to this definition, the phrase denotes land, buildings and structures owned by an entrepreneur or other entity engaged in business activity. An exception is provided[42]:

1. residential buildings and the land associated with these buildings,
2. certain land under water and
3. buildings, structures or parts thereof which have been ordered to be demolished.

These situations are so rare that, in practice, any object of taxation that would be in the entrepreneur's possession would be associated with business activity. This was opposed by the Constitutional Tribunal in its verdict of 24 February 2021,[43] which stated that this regulation (understood such that the connection of land, a building or a structure with the conducting of business activity is determined exclusively by the possession of the land, the building or the structure by the entrepreneur or another entity conducting business activity) is inconsistent with the Polish Constitution. In response to this judgement, the jurisprudence of administrative courts clearly tends to decide whether a given object is associated with conducting business activity based on whether a given object is treated by an entrepreneur as their business property—that is, in some way connected with their business activity. This association may be determined by whether the object is subject to depreciation under the provisions on income taxes (but remember that in Poland, for example, land is not subject to depreciation).[44]

[41] Article 1a(3), L.T.C.A.

[42] Article 1a(2a), L.T.C.A.

[43] SK 39/19.

[44] Judgement of the Supreme Administrative Court of 15 December 2021, III FSK 4061 21.

Chapter 3
The Taxation of Assets Used to Extract Energy Resources

Abstract The problem concerning the taxation of the facilities used to extract energy resources is most often (apart from lignite mines) linked to how the term 'underground excavation' is understood. Only the objects located in an excavation site can be taxed, not an excavation itself. As a result, the cost of conducting an excavation itself should not be included in the taxable objects' value. Excavation equipment is quite complex, which results in difficulties separating the taxable construction part from the equipment. This problem is typical of the Polish real estate tax.

Keywords Hard coal mine · Lignite mine · Crude oil mine · Gas mine · Real estate tax · Underground excavation

3.1 Hard Coal Mines

3.1.1 Hard Coal Mines in Poland: An Introduction

Hard coal mines in Poland are exclusively deep mines. Geological conditions make mining hard coal impossible using the open-pit method (as in Australia).

Poland's hard coal mining facilities (or, more precisely, complexes of facilities) are quite intricate, with even several thousand employees working at them.[1] Such complexes of facilities are used not only to extract coal from underground but also to process and load the extracted coal.

The description of one mine is useful as an example, and for this purpose we have selected the Bogdanka Coal Mine. It operates within the 'Puchaczów V' mining area, which spans about 73 km^2. This area contains 18 balance seams of hard coal (at depths of 650–730 m), but only eight seams qualify for exploitation presently. The Bogdanka mine's mining area is divided into three exploitation regions: the main region in Bogdanka and peripheral regions in Nadrybie and Stefanów. Each region

[1] Employment in Poland's only active hard coal mine outside of Upper Silesia, the Bogdanka Coal Mine, has exceeded 4,000 workers over the last decade. See https://www.lw.com.pl/pl,2,s338,pracownicy.html. Retrieved: 30.06.2022.

W. Morawski and A. Kałążny, *The Taxation of Energy-Sector Assets: Polish Tax Legislation on the Eve of Energy Transformation*, SpringerBriefs in Energy,
https://doi.org/10.1007/978-3-031-15673-1_3

contains two shafts: an intake shaft and a ventilation shaft. The mine also has two hoisting shafts equipped with skip hoisting equipment in Bogdanka and a newer hoisting shaft, implemented in 2011, in Stefanów.

The main mining region, the Bogdanka Area, comprises:

- main shafts (Pit Shaft 1.2—an intake, material and transportation shaft with a diameter of φ 6.0 m and a depth of 995 m—and Production Shaft 1.3, an exhaust shaft with a diameter of φ 7.5 m and a depth of 1030 m),
- a set of two main fans at Production Shaft 1.3,
- a coal preparation plant,
- a waste rock dumping site,
- administrative, office and social buildings and
- a warehouse complex.[2]

A mine comprises an above-ground portion and an underground portion. The above-ground portion consists essentially of buildings and technical equipment, the taxation of which—obviously—raises serious problems, but such concerns are typical for the taxation of industrial facilities. However, a mine's underground portions have been subject to heated disputes (lasting for several years). Such underground portions contain the excavation operations, which employ the technical equipment used to extract coal and maintain a mine. Given of the underground facilities' enormous value, this dispute was very important for both mining companies and the municipalities in which mines are located.

3.1.2 The Specificity of the Legal Regulation of Mining Activities

Mining is such a specific type of human activity that, in Poland, the construction of mining facilities is not only regulated by the C.L.A. but also, traditionally, by separate legislation which covers all aspects of mining activity (from mineral exploration to mine construction and exploitation); in its current form, this traditional legislation is embodied in the Act of 9 June 2011—the geological and mining law.[3] According to Article 2(1) of the C.L.A., this act does not apply to excavations. At the same time, according to Article 2(2)(1) of the C.L.A., 'the provisions of this Act are without prejudice to separate provisions, and in particular […] the Geological and Mining Law—with respect to construction objects of mining plants'. Pursuant to Article 6(1)(4) of the G.M.L.A., a construction object of a mining plant is,

[2] https://www.lw.com.pl/pl,2,s170,charakterystyka_ogolna.html. Retrieved: 30 June 2022.

[3] Journal of Laws No. 163, item 981—hereinafter the 'geological and mining law act' or 'G.M.L.A.' When some of the disputes analysed below were taking place, the Geological and Mining Law Act of 4 February 1994 was in force. However, we do not analyse it in this book since the change in legal regulation did not significantly practically influence the problem of taxing underground mine operations.

> a construction object of a mining plant located outside an underground excavation, which is a construction object within the meaning of the Act of 7 July 1994—the Construction Law [. . .],[4] used directly for conducting activities regulated by the Act in the scope of extraction of minerals from deposits, and in underground mining plants extracting hard coal together with preparation of extracted minerals for sale, underground storage of substances without tanks or underground storage of waste, remaining in technological relation with extraction of a mineral.

Article 6(1)(6) of the G.M.L.A. defines an *underground waste storage* site as 'a part of the rock mass, including an underground excavation, used to dispose of waste by depositing it'. An *excavation*, on the other hand, is 'a space in a land property or rock mass resulting from mining works' (G.M.L.A., Article 6[1][17]), and a *mining site* is,

> a technically and organisationally separated group of means used directly to perform activities regulated by the Act with respect to extraction of minerals from deposits, and in underground mining plants extracting hard coal together with preparation of the extracted mineral for sale, underground storage of substances without a tank, or underground storage of waste remaining in a technological connection with the extraction of the mineral, including mining excavations, construction objects, devices and installation. (G.M.L.A., Article 16[1][18])

3.1.3 The Dispute Over the Taxation of Underground Excavations in Poland

The dispute on the taxation of underground excavations has been the subject of many, often divergent judgements by administrative courts. This dispute can be divided into several periods with different approaches to the problem of taxing underground excavation. After the L.T.C.A.'s entry into force (until 31 December 2002, when the legal regulation was differed from the current regulation, since the scope of appeals to the C.L.A. was much narrower), at first, excavations were not taxed in practice. However, when the disputes reached the administrative courts, some Polish courts' rulings presented a different position.[5] The resolutions of the Supreme Administrative Court of 2 July 2001[6] and of the Supreme Court of 12 March 2002[7] presented different views—namely, that underground excavations are not subject to the real estate tax. This was accompanied by doctrinal disputes (Brzeziński & Kalinowski, 2001, pp. 79–85), (Hanusz, 2001, pp. 20–28), (Etel, 2002, pp. 77–84), (Mastalski, 2001, pp. 37–39).

---

[4] C.L.A.

[5] Resolution of the Supreme Administrative Court of 29 November 1999, FPK 3/99. We do not analyse the legal regulation at that time in this book, which—in our view—differed little from the present regulation. The Supreme Administrative Court resolution is more significant than an 'ordinary' Supreme Administrative Court judgement. Other courts must generally apply the view contained in the resolution (though some exceptions have applied).

[6] FPS 2/01.

[7] III ZP 34/01.

After a thorough amendment to the L.T.C.A. on 1 January 2003,[8] municipalities' hopes that underground excavations would be taxable were revived, a view which was the administrative courts initially accepted. Another clear caesura in time was the judgement of the Constitutional Tribunal of 13 September 2011.[9] The administrative courts' judgements issued after Tribunal judgement are very restrictive regarding the possibility to tax even the equipment located at excavation sites, negating—of course—the taxation of an excavation itself. The dispute over taxation of mines was so difficult to resolve that even the subject of the dispute was itself disputed. The courts decided on the taxation of underground excavations, but what 'underground excavations' actually entailed was unclear since the parties to the dispute seemed to understand the term differently.

In mining, an 'underground excavation' is understood to be a void in the ground left after the extraction of a mineral. This understanding of an 'underground excavation' is referred to in the statutory definition in Article 6(1)(17) of the G.M.L.A. Of course, in this sense, an excavation is not a structure (or a construction object at all) because it is simply a void.

The administrative courts' jurisprudence—particularly before the judgement of the Constitutional Tribunal of 13 September 2011[10]—presented a different concept of an underground excavation. The prevailing view was that,

> also an excavation, for the purposes of real estate tax, should not be treated as a homogenous object, but as a structure consisting of individual objects (devices) functionally connected with each other, i.e. shafts, adits, power lines, etc., serving—generally speaking—to extract minerals. The aforementioned facilities and equipment constitute a component part of an excavation used for conducting economic activity and it is on these facilities (equipment) that the real estate tax should be charged'.[11]

In another case, the Supreme Administrative Court upheld a ruling by the Provincial Administrative Court which accepted the municipality's position that 'construction and engineering facilities, such as ventilation and drainage pipelines, pumping stations, conveyors, loading stations, railway tracks, telephone and power lines with transformer stations' are subject to the real estate tax.[12] However, already quoting the text of the Provincial Administrative Court judgement, which was the subject of a cessation appeal, the Supreme Administrative Court mentioned, 'shafts, adits, power lines, etc.'., which would be the components of an excavation. Unfortunately, in justifying its position, the Supreme Administrative Court did not refer in any way to the issue of understanding the phrase 'underground excavation', and in the last part of the justification, the Supreme Administrative Court stated that, 'the dispute in the case centred around the determination of the subject of real estate tax, namely whether this subject includes, inter alia, structures or parts thereof [...] located in an

[8] At this point, the L.T.C.A. essentially took on its current form.

[9] P 33/09.

[10] P 33/09.

[11] Judgement of the Provincial Administrative Court in Wrocław of 15 March 2007, I SA/Wr 1814/06.

[12] Judgement of the Supreme Administrative Court of 3 February 2006, II FSK 656/05.

underground excavation'. This phrasing would imply that only structures located in an underground excavation site would be subject to taxation, not the underground excavation itself. Unfortunately, more judgements have addressed the problem of determining what is actually in dispute. Thus, a view emerged that an excavation is not a void in a rock mass but the entirety of a mine's underground structures. This perspective, therefore, justified excavations' taxation.

Additional confusion has stemmed from how assets are recorded in registers kept by entrepreneurs. In Poland, entrepreneurs keep records of their fixed assets, which serve—among other purposes—to calculate depreciation deductions, which are deducted from income for income tax purposes. These records are based on the classification of fixed assets (KŚT), which does not specify 'mining excavations' but only includes such objects under Group 2, Subgroup 20, Type 200: 'Construction for mining and quarrying'. Whether this type of fixed asset also includes excavations is unclear. However, in practice, when valuing this fixed asset, the cost of creating an excavation has been included in its value. This method of recordkeeping derives from rules which, at one time, were introduced by the Ministry of Industry and Trade in the form of an 'instruction on the rules of classification and financing of mining structures (excavations) in hard coal mines'.[13] Obviously, this circumstance could not be relevant to the decision on the taxation rules for underground excavation. However, over the course of disputes on the taxation of underground excavation, tax authorities and the administrative courts following them uncritically accepted the classification of assets on the basis of the KŚT and—without exception –considered that all facilities classified by taxpayers as Type 200 of the KŚT constitute 'structures' as per the meaning in the L.T.C.A. This acceptance seems to partly explain the problems in determining the subject of the real estate tax by tax authorities and courts throughout the dispute pending over excavations. It explains these problems because, by relying—incorrectly—on the nomenclature created (among other nomenclatures) for statistical purposes, using the term 'structure' in relation to underground excavations and classifying these objects as Type 200 of the KŚT, taxation was indeed imposed on excavations (i.e., the costs of excavating a 'hole in the ground'), even if the courts claimed that only structures in the underground excavation site were subject to taxation and that underground excavation operations themselves were not.

The above issue of taxation of mine (underground excavation) was subject to a particularly thorough analysis in the above-quoted judgement of the Constitutional Tribunal of 13 September 2011.[14] Referring strictly to the problem of taxing underground excavations, the tribunal stated (in Item 4.4.1. of the judgement's justification) that it is,

> the thesis, repeated in many judgements and being a paraphrase of the position formulated in the doctrine, according to which an excavation, for the purposes of real estate taxation, should be treated not as a homogenous object but as a structure consisting of many objects

[13] Letter from the Undersecretary of State in the Ministry of Industry and Trade of 13 June 1995, No. DE-2/AM/3456/95.

[14] P 33/09.

> and construction devices (e.g. shafts, adits, shafts, pipelines, power and ventilation lines), connected to a number of buildings and construction equipment.

This thesis was expressed because the jurisprudence used to assume that a mine's workings were not a homogenous object but a structure comprising a number of objects and construction devices (e.g., shafts, adits, shafts, pipelines, and power and ventilation lines) which are functionally connected to each other so as to enable the extraction of mineral resources. The jurisprudence assumed that the above 'facilities and equipment are to constitute parts of an excavation as a structure serving to conduct economic activity, and real estate tax should be calculated on their value'. In formulating this position, the administrative courts maintained, at the same time, that an 'excavation' (understood in accordance with Article 6(17) of the G.M.L.A.) was a space in a land property or in a rock mass, but all of the facilities and equipment that constitute an excavation as a structure are not subject to taxation.

The Constitutional Tribunal stated,

> Notwithstanding the fact that neither the provisions of the G.M.L.A., the C.L.A. nor, still less, the provisions of the L.T.C.A. provide any basis for constructing and using a different definition of the expression 'excavation' than the legal definition contained in the M.G.L.A, the view under consideration, because of its generality, ambiguity and possibly also internal contradiction, may lead to incorrect determination of the subject of the real estate tax and thus to incorrect determination of the basis for this taxation.

Referring only to the strictly understood issue of taxing underground excavations, the Constitutional Tribunal summarised its considerations as follows:

> Firstly, there should be no doubt that excavations conceived in accordance with the G.M.L.A. as spaces in land properties or in rock masses, not being structures, cannot be subject to real estate tax as such structures: neither independently (as excavation in the physical sense) nor together with the equipment located in them (as excavation in the comprehensive sense). Adoption of the opposite view would be tantamount to constitutionally impermissible broadening interpretation of the tax regulation.

> Secondly, excavations in the technical sense, i.e. sets of functionally connected devices for the extraction of minerals, located in spaces in the land or in rock masses created as a result of mining works, may potentially be subject to real estate tax as construction objects, provided that such sets may be qualified as construction objects in the form of structures within the meaning of the C.L.A, which are structures within the meaning of the L.T.C.A., which requires, however, that the units in question be assigned to one of the names of structures *expressis verbis* listed in the construction law. It should be borne in mind that even if one were to allow, by way of analogy, for mine workings in the technical sense to be regarded as structures within the meaning of the C.L.A., the name 'excavation' denoting a type of structure does not appear in this Act. It should also be emphasised that the distinction of the technical term of a mine workings in the light of the provisions of the G.M.L.A. does not appear justified and may lead to numerous misunderstandings and consequently it should be abandoned, the more so as it is sufficient and clear to distinguish two issues: taxation of excavations within the meaning of the G.M.L.A. and taxation of installations situated in such excavations.

It follows quite unambiguously that an 'underground excavation', understood as a space in a rock mass, cannot be subject to taxation. The Constitutional Tribunal expressed its position by formulating the thesis of the judgement as follows:

> Article 2(1)(3) in connection with Article 1a(1)(2) of the Local Taxes and Charges Act of 12 January 1991 ...[. . .], understood in such a way that it does not refer to underground excavations and may refer to facilities and equipment located in those excavations, is consistent with the principle of statutory determinacy of tax regulations and the principle of correct legislation derived from Article 217 in connection with Article 84 and Article 2 of the Constitution of the Republic of Poland.

The Constitutional Tribunal clearly separates the issues of taxing an excavation and taxing the objects located in an excavation site. In relation to the latter potentially taxable object, the Constitutional Tribunal's position is very cautious.

3.1.4 The Taxable Underground Portions of a Mine

After the Constitutional Tribunal's judgement of 13 September 2011, the dispute over taxation of mines revolved around the problem of 'matching' objects located in an excavation site with the specific names of structures that in the C.L.A. No major doubts suggested that this treatment could be applied, inter alia, to certain pipelines, the rails of railways located underground, et cetera. These objects have 'above-ground' counterparts. If such an object is taxed when it is above ground, it should also be taxed when it is underground.

In practice, most disputes have involved the taxation of underground mining supports. These structures are not explicitly named as 'structures' in the C.L.A. regulations. However, the jurisprudence has formed the view that 'the linguistic interpretation of the term 'retaining structure' referred to in Article 3(3) of the Act of 7 July 1994 construction law [...], supplemented by an external systemic interpretation, allows mining supports to be qualified as retaining structures'.[15] The Supreme Administrative Court explained in another judgement:

> the task of the mining support is to counteract the pressure of the rocks surrounding the interior of the excavation (maintaining stability). Mining supports ensure the stability of the rock mass in which underground excavations are created. An important feature of the mining support is that it resists the pressure of the rock masses. The purpose of the mining support is therefore the same as that of a retaining structure. Retaining structures are independent structures and can successfully fulfil their role without the need to install separate equipment in them'.[16]

This position is widely accepted in jurisprudence. However, this acceptance did not mean the end of the problems of taxation of mines. For instance, elements recognised as structures are usually not separate, depreciable fixed assets. Usually, a single fixed asset comprises both the value of mining supports (as well as other facilities located in the excavation site) and the costs of conducting an excavation.[17] However,

[15] Judgement of the Supreme Administrative Court of 9 August 2018, II FSK 2058/16.

[16] Judgement of the Supreme Administrative Court of 20 April 2022, III FSK 456/21.

[17] Such separate, fixed assets may include more examples. An entrepreneur building the subsequent elements of an excavation site or equipping it with such subsequent elements may create subsequent fixed assets, the value of which would include expenses for subsequent investments.

the costs of excavation cannot be included in the tax base. As a result, the initial value of the fixed asset cannot be the tax base for the structure, since this value would mean that the excavation would also be taxed. Making a percentage division of the value of the fixed asset into the taxable portion (e.g., the mining support) and the non-taxable portion (e.g., the costs of excavation) is impossible. Jurisprudence has generally accepted that, in such a case, the structure's market value would be the taxable base. This market value would, of course, be the value as of the date upon which the tax obligation arose. In the case of a mine, this view may mean that a structure's market value from many years ago must be applied.[18] The practice of experts appointed by the tax authorities has raised many objections. Their valuation methods lead to results that sometimes astonish taxpayers. Quite simple construction elements have proven to have a disproportionately high share in the value of an entire fixed asset. An administrative court may theoretically ensure the correctness of an expert's method of assessing the value of the tax base, but in practice, this control is very difficult since the court does not generally conduct evidentiary proceedings.

3.2 Lignite Mines

In Poland, lignite mines are exclusively opencast mines. Given the characteristics of this raw material, its extraction in deep mines would be irrational.

From a legal point of view, an opencast mine is also essentially a mining excavation, like a deep mine. However, it is a pit on the surface of the Earth. At the same time, it has a less complicated structure since, at first glance, it simply resembles a 'hole in the ground'.[19] Due to lignite's characteristics, the mine is closely connected to its power station, which burns coal almost continuously.

Despite the fact that a lignite mine is an excavation and must be 'built', nobody has suggested that it should be taxed as a structure. The pit is taxable, but as land—not as a structure.[20]

This does not mean that no facilities on the mine site can be taxed. Of course, any buildings, roads, power lines et cetera will be taxed. Usually, the problem with opencast mines is getting rid of excess water. Costly dewatering installations—which include wells with powered pumps, power cables, control equipment et cetera—are not listed in the C.L.A. as structures. However, they can be taxed in part as

[18] The problem is complicated by the fact that, for more than 20 years, the taxation of these facilities has been under dispute, so entrepreneurs did not establish structures' market value for the purpose of calculating the real estate tax. Even when the dispute was resolved, many entrepreneurs applied simplified methods (which were, unfortunately, not compliant with the L.T.C.A.) to determine the value of the tax base (e.g. determining the percentage of taxed objects' value to the total fixed asset).

[19] The Bełchatów lignite mine is quite commonly referred to as the biggest hole in the ground in Poland. It is over 12 km long and 200 m deep. See https://www.national-geographic.pl/traveler/artykul/polska-dla-ciekawskich-belchatow-najwieksza-dziura-w-ziemi, retrieved 30 June 2022.

[20] Regarding gravel mines, this view was expressed by the Provincial Administrative Court in Łódź in its judgement of 20 June 2013, I SA/Łd 295/13. This view is also valid for lignite mines.

'construction parts of technical equipment', a view which—of course—generates the problem of separating this portion from the whole facility.

As the issue of environmental protection becomes more and more important, facilities built—for example—to limit dust emissions or underground screens in order to counteract the fall in groundwater levels in areas adjacent to an opencast mine can become an increasing problem. Such objects are, to be sure, 'constructional' in nature in a sense since they are made of building products. However, more often than not, finding a name for a type of construction that would include these objects in the C.L.A. would be difficult. Because of the prohibition on analogy,[21] taxing them with the real estate tax would be difficult, even though their inclusion would be logical.

Somewhat surprisingly, the jurisprudence database of Polish administrative courts includes no judgements at all concerning the taxation of opencast lignite mines. This omission may be due to the fact that only five of these mines are located in Poland (including one which is being liquidated).

3.3 Crude Oil Mines and Gas Mines

Oil and gas mines may, of course, can differ from each other, but they can be analysed together because their taxation principles are identical.

Both mine types' main element is a borehole. Boreholes are a type of excavation under Polish law. In the context of the judgement of the Constitutional Tribunal of 13 September 2011 (P 33/09), they are not structures. However, facilities located in such excavation sites may be structures. In the case of hard coal mines, the jurisprudence of Polish administrative courts has accepted that mining supports are retaining constructions and are, therefore, subject to the real estate tax. This principle should similarly apply to boreholes. Admittedly, no up-to-date judgements from the administrative courts resolve this issue, but the jurisprudence on salt mines (when salt is extracted by rinsing it out with water) can be applied analogously to this context. The Provincial Administrative Court in Bydgoszcz's judgement of 22 January 2019[22] states:

> it should be assumed that the preliminary, guide and technical columns, located in a borehole, constitute a retaining structure referred to in Article 3(3) of the C.L.A., as their function is to protect (casing) the borehole against the pressure of the ground and rocks in order to enable the safe extraction of rock salt. It is irrelevant whether they perform the function of casing only (pre-column) or whether, in addition to their casing function, they also perform the other functions indicated above.

In the case of oil and gas wells, all the elements that prevent the well from being buried by rock could undoubtedly be treated as support structures (these elements would include guide pipe columns, cement casing and production pipe columns).

---

[21] Judgement of Constitutional Tribunal of 13 September 2011, P 33/09.

[22] I SA/Bd 940/18.

Treating production pipes in the same way would be rather difficult because their sole function is to extract gas.

Both oil and gas mines also have an above-ground section. In the case of a gas mine, this above-ground section includes a methanol addition device, a flow measurement venturi, a so-called siphoning venturi and measuring equipment. In principle, these devices should be regarded as technical equipment. Their purpose is the pre-treatment of raw material. Similarly, any control equipment (pressure gauges etc.) cannot be regarded as structures.

Chapter 4
The Taxation of Assets Used to Transport and Store Energy Resources

Abstract The assets used to transport and store energy raw materials (at the moment, mainly oil and gas) generate a significant tax burden because many of them are taxable construction objects that—due to their high unit value (tanks) or scale (pipelines running across the whole country)—are very highly valuable, which translates into a high tax base. At the same time, some areas in this respect are disputable, and such disputes' resolution for the tax authorities' benefit additionally increases this already high tax burden (the treatment of the accompanying infrastructure as an element of the structure and the treatment of tanks with the features of buildings as structures). This cost is not present in the case of renewable energy, which—by its very nature—does not require any infrastructure for the storage or transportation of energy resources. Therefore, due to the nature of Polish real estate tax regulations, renewable energy can be said to be doubly competitive with fossil energy Firstly, traditional energy requires expenditures on the construction of infrastructure to transport and store energy resources. And secondly, these expenditures largely increase the real estate tax base.

Keywords Pipeline · Oil tank · Gas tank · LNG · FSRU · Gas reduction and measurement station

4.1 Pipelines Used to Transport Oil and Gas

4.1.1 The Tax Treatment of Pipelines

The definition of a 'structure' in Article 3(3) of the C.L.A. (to which the L.T.C.A. indirectly refers in its definition of a structure subject to real estate tax) indicates, as an example (among others) of a structure, linear objects. Pursuant to the definition provided in Article 3(3a) of the C.L.A., a linear object includes, inter alia, a gas pipeline and a pipeline. Although an oil pipeline is not literally mentioned in the definition of a 'linear object' in the same way as a gas pipeline, it should be deemed to

W. Morawski and A. Kałążny, *The Taxation of Energy-Sector Assets: Polish Tax Legislation on the Eve of Energy Transformation*, SpringerBriefs in Energy,
https://doi.org/10.1007/978-3-031-15673-1_4

fall within the meaning of the term 'pipeline' as used in this provision. Consequently, both a gas pipeline and an oil pipeline are subject to the real estate tax as structures.

In the past, according to Article 7(1) (5) of the L.T.C.A. in its original wording (in force since the act came into force; Journal of Laws 1991, No. 9, item 31), gas and fuel pipelines (among others) were exempted from the real estate tax. Subsequently, as of 1 January 1997, this exemption from the real estate tax was applicable to, inter alia, gas and fuel distribution pipelines and lines.[1] This exemption was fully eliminated as of 1 January 2001 by virtue of the Act of 13 October 2000[2] on amending the act on the revenues of local self-government units in 1999 and 2000 and certain other acts. According to the justification of the amendments to the provisions, the reason to liquidate the exemption in question was the need to increase municipalities' tax revenues (Kałążny, 2020b, p. 155).

4.1.2 Associated Infrastructures

Although the taxation of pipelines as structures is not controversial in the current legal regulation, numerous disputes between taxpayers and tax authorities have arisen in last decade over the classification of infrastructure that accompanies pipelines, including—in particular—gas reduction and measurement station facilities as described below.

In the tax authorities' opinion, the technical devices for gas reduction and metring stations located both in containers placed on foundations and in cabinets on buildings' walls constitute a technical and utility whole, which ensures the use of the gas network in accordance with its purpose. Moreover, the tax authorities opine that, because the facilities' disconnection would result in the gas pipeline's inability to function, these facilities should be treated from a tax perspective in the same way as a gas pipeline; thus, their value should increase the tax base for structures. Such a position would entail a significant increase in pipeline owners' tax burden because gas reduction and measurement station facilities are relatively valuable objects.

The jurisprudence has formed a favourable position for taxpayers, rejecting this argument by tax authorities as unsupported by regulations. In the opinion of the Supreme Administrative Court,[3] in order to consider the issue of the possible tax classification of gas reduction and measurement stations, a statement that a gas pipeline and a reduction and measurement station constitute two separate objects from the perspective of the construction law is crucial. These objects are also made using separate technologies. For these reasons, the Supreme Administrative Court holds that gas reduction and measurement station facilities cannot be classified as structures subject to the real estate tax. At the same time, the Supreme Administrative Court pointed out that Article 3(3) of the C.L.A., which catalogues structures that

[1] Journal of Laws 1996, No. 91, item 409.

[2] Journal of Laws 2000 No. 95, item 1041.

[3] E.g. the judgement of the Supreme Administrative Court of 27 March 2017, II FSK 311/15.

may be subject to real estate tax, lists—among other things—the building portions of technical equipment. For this reason, while the gas reduction and measurement equipment itself does not constitute a structure, its constructional portion (e.g. the casing in which the equipment is located or the foundation upon which it is placed) can constitute such a structure.

In this context, we must point to the most recent Supreme Administrative Court jurisprudence relating to technical equipment connected to the electricity network, according to which equipment such as transformers constitutes structures because it ensures the use of the network for its intended purpose (for more on this topic, see Sect. 10.2.1: 'The Tax Qualification of Transformer Station Structures'). So far, these theses have not been transferred to judgements concerning the tax qualification of gas reduction and measurement stations, but such a transfer is easy to imagine. Gas reduction facilities play a similar role in relation to the gas network as transformers in relation to the power network. Their task is to reduce gas pressure from high to medium or from medium to low (which is analogous to transformers' reduction of electrical currents' voltage). Therefore, we should point out that despite the formation of the line of jurisprudence favourable for taxpayers—excluding equipment for gas reduction and measurement stations from the scope of taxation—contrary positions in the jurisprudence cannot be ruled out.

Similar conclusions to the case of the infrastructure that accompanies gas pipelines may be drawn with respect to similar facilities connected to oil pipelines. As technical devices, they should—in principle—be treated as beyond the scope of the real estate tax. However, similar to the jurisprudence concerning gas reduction devices and transformers, the jurisprudential perspective in this respect is not very stable.

4.1.3 The Soil Beneath Pipelines

Pipelines that transport energy resources can affect the taxation of the land over (or under) which they run. In particular, the recognition that such land is occupied for commercial activities could involve a significant increase in the tax burden paid for the land.

As the law currently stands (pursuant to Article 1a[2a][4] of the L.T.C.A.), land occupied by transmission facilities that form part of an enterprise engaged, inter alia, in the transmission or distribution of liquids and gases or transporting extracted natural gas or crude oil (as well as the land occupied by process belts and protective zones around such facilities) is not deemed to be connected to the pursuit of business activities—with the exception of land held by the transmission entrepreneur in their own right, perpetual usufruct or owned by them.

The topic of taxing the land under oil and gas pipelines has generally not been addressed in the jurisprudence of administrative courts. Meanwhile, in the past, numerous disputes in this respect have concerned a similar case (i.e. the land under power lines).[4] For more extensive commentary on these disputes and possible doubts regarding the treatment of land under the current legislation, see Sect. 10.3: 'The Land under Transmission Lines'.

4.2 Liquefied Natural Gas Terminals

Liquefied Natural Gas (hereinafter LNG) terminals are an important element of the Polish natural gas supply system (the existing onshore terminal located in Świnoujście, as well as the planned Floating Storage Regasification Unit, hereinafter the 'FSRU'). They enable the off-take and regasification of liquefied gas delivered by sea. From a tax perspective, both types of LNG terminals should be considered separately due to their different constructions, which result in different qualifications for the real estate tax. Similar conclusions to the case of onshore LNG terminals will also apply to a terminal receiving crude oil (the oil port located in Gdansk).[5]

4.2.1 Onshore Liquefied Natural Gas Terminals

An onshore LNG terminal is not a single facility but a set of many different facilities that make up one functional whole, just like—for example—a production plant or a power plant. The technological processes currently operated by the LNG terminal include unloading LNG from a tanker at the unloading wharf, the in-process storage of LNG in tanks, the regasification of LNG and dispatching the gas to the transmission system (pipelines) and loading the LNG onto tankers.[6] Consequently, from the tax perspective, a proper approach is not to treat such a group of assets as a single subject of the real estate tax but, rather, to determine which of the objects that comprise the group meets the definition of a 'building' or a 'structure' and to tax them accordingly. The remaining components of the terminal, since they do not constitute either a building or a structure, will be beyond the scope of the real estate tax.

Note that this approach has been the subject of disputes between taxpayers and tax authorities, as described below. Since these disputes have not yet specifically concerned LNG terminals, to illustrate the problem, we will refer to the jurisprudence concerning sewage treatment plants. According to some tax authorities, the separate tax treatment of individual components of a sewage treatment plant (buildings, tanks, technical equipment etc.) is artificial and unjustified because a sewage treatment plant is directly mentioned in the definition of a 'structure' in Article 3.3 C.L.A. Consequently, according to proponents of this approach, all assets constituting the

---

[4] Judgement of the Supreme Administrative Court of 9 June 2016, II FSK 1156/14.

[5] https://naftoport.pl/, retrieved 23 May 2022.

[6] https://terminallng.gaz-system.pl/pl/terminal-lng/terminal-lng-w-swinoujsciu/, retrieved 23 May 2022.

so-called technical and utilitarian whole in the form of the sewage treatment plant should be classified as a structure and taxed on their value. Potentially, a similar argument could be applied to elements of the LNG terminal, which could be regarded, for example, as a freestanding industrial installation—which, similar to a sewage treatment plant, is listed in Article 3.3 of the C.L.A. as an example of a structure. We emphasise, however, that such a tax classification would generate a much higher tax burden than the separate classification of individual components because some of them may meet the definition of a 'building' (the tax base for which is its area, and not its value, an approach that often generates a lower tax base), while others do not constitute structures at all (various types of technical equipment). The Supreme Administrative Court ruled against the concept of a 'single large structure' and, in its rulings relating to sewage treatment plants, pointed out.

> that the functional connection between various structures forming a complex of sewage treatment plants (or other structures listed in Article 3(3) C.L.A.) cannot prejudge the fact that this is a single structure which should be included in only one of the categories of taxable objects listed in Article 2(1)(1) and (2) L.T.C.A.

Consequently, the court correctly held regarding the complex of a sewage pre-treatment plant that facilities, together with their accompanying equipment—which are connected to one another in performing the function of sewage pre-treatment, which constitute a technical and utilitarian whole implementing that technological process and which do not at the same time constitute a building—should be regarded as a structure. This portion of the sewage pre-treatment plant is subject to taxation as a structure, for which the taxable base is the value. On the other hand, a building which—despite forming part of a sewage treatment plant in that it directly performs the functions of the plant—nevertheless does not cease to possess the aforementioned characteristics of a building should constitute a separate object of taxation as a building, for which the basis of taxation is its surface area.[7]

The above-cited jurisprudence resolves the issue of the buildings included in the terminal—they should be treated as separate objects taxed on their usable area. In this context, an important issue is the tax qualification of LNG tanks, which could meet the definition of a 'building'. A more extensive commentary on this subject is provided later in this chapter (see Sect. 4.3: 'Oil and Gas Tanks').

A separate issue is the tax treatment of a number of different types of technical equipment, enabling the performance of specific processes within the terminal—particularly gas unloading and loading equipment and regasification installations. In principle, technical equipment is beyond the scope of the real estate tax due directly to the definition of a 'structure' set out in Article 3.3 of the C.L.A. This definition indicates that only the building portions of technical equipment may be treated as structures. Nevertheless, as we indicated earlier in this chapter (see Sect. 4.1.2: 'Associated Infrastructures'), technical facilities connected to a gas network risk qualifying as a part of the structure on the basis of the definition of a 'construction object', according to which such facilities in particular are structures, together

[7] Judgement of the Supreme Administrative Court of 28 September 2017, II FSK 2221/15.

with installations that ensure the possibility of their use in accordance with their purpose. This risk seems significantly lower for LNG terminal facilities than for facilities directly connected to the gas network, such as gas reduction and measurement stations. Indeed, the 'gas network'—understood as a system of gas pipelines for gas transmission—may function regardless of whether it is connected to the regasification installation at the LNG terminal. The terminal should be considered not an element of the gas network but one of the gas sources that the network distributes. The LNG terminal may be said to perform a function in relation to the gas network, similar to the function of a power plant in relation to the power network—it supplies the network with gas (or, in a power plant's case, electricity) but is not a necessary element for the network to perform its transmission function.

Additionally, we should point out that a significant part of the investments in the LNG terminal is port infrastructure constructions, such as quays or jetties, carried out together with the Szczecin and Świnoujście Seaport Authority.[8] Note that the L.T.C.A. provides a tax exemption for port infrastructure constructions, so this part of the LNG terminal should—in principle—be beyond the scope of taxation (Kałążny, 2020c, pp. 50–55).

The LNG terminal in Świnoujście is currently one of the highest generators of real estate tax to the budget of one municipality in Poland. At the moment, the annual tax paid to the Świnoujście budget from the taxable objects included in the LNG terminal amounts to about 40 million PLN.[9] At the same time, the cost incurred so far for the construction of the terminal is about 2.8 billion PLN.[10] A comparison of these amounts reveals that over two-thirds of the total investment expenditures were treated as taxable constructions (assuming that the buildings within the terminal are relatively few in number and relatively low in value) and, considering that part of the expenditures—as indicated above in this chapter—qualify for the port infrastructure exemption, this percentage may be even higher. From this perspective, the LNG terminal should be considered a very high real-estate-tax-generating project. For the City of Świnoujście, whose total real estate tax revenues, according to the data for 2022, are about 80 million PLN,[11] the tax revenues from the terminal contribute as much as half of the city's total real estate tax revenues.

4.2.2 The Floating Storage and Regasification Unit Terminal

The second type of LNG terminal present in Poland (though currently at the planning stage as of May 2022) is a floating terminal, the so-called FSRU. It is a tanker-type

[8] https://businessinsider.com.pl/firmy/zarzadzanie/wykonawcy-rozbudowy-terminala-lng-w-swinoujsciu-za-19-mld-zl/rjwmc0m, retrieved 23 May 2022.

[9] https://twojeradio.fm/jeszcze-wieksze-pieniadze-z-gazoportu-w-swinoujsciu-wplyna-do-kasy-miasta.html, retrieved 23 May 2022.

[10] https://inzynieria.com/uploaded/magazines/pdf/pe01_pierwszy_polski_terminal_lng.pdfaccessed, retrieved 23 May 2022.

[11] https://bip.um.swinoujscie.pl/uchwala/33215/uchwala-nr-lvi-452-2021 retrieved 23 May 2022.

vessel used to transport liquid LNG, together with a regasification module. This type of unit is, in principle, permanently moored at a distance of several kilometres from the port, and it performs the same role as the land-based LNG terminal—that is, it ensures the storage of imported LNG and its subsequent regasification and supply of natural gas to the network.[12] As we indicated above in Sect. 4.2.1., the onshore LNG terminal generates a very significant amount of real estate tax, significantly improving the financial standing of the municipality where it is located. It should be considered if a similar case may occur for the FSRU?

The FSRU, in order to be subject to the real estate tax, would have to meet the definition of a 'building' or 'structure' in the L.T.C.A. No one disputes that the FSRU does not meet the definition of a 'building' due to its lack of a permanent connection to the land and its lack of foundations (despite being permanently moored in a specific location, it remains a vessel). Therefore, whether the FSRU meets the definition of a 'structure' on the grounds of the L.T.C.A.—that is, whether it constitutes a 'construction object' within the meaning of the provisions of the construction law as neither a 'building' nor a 'small architecture object'—or a 'construction device' within the meaning of the provisions of the construction law related to a 'construction object' (Article 3(1) of the C.L.A.) (which ensures the possibility of using the object in accordance with its purpose) remains to be considered.

First, we should point out that the FSRU does not constitute a construction object because it was not built using construction materials but manufactured in a shipyard. On the other hand, according to the Supreme Administrative Court jurisprudence, equipment made in manufacturing facilities is not considered a construction object.[13]

At the same time, the catalogue of structures provided in Article 3(3) of the C.L.A., which may be subject to the real estate tax, does not include categories to which the FSRU could at least be similar. The only category that may require deeper analysis is the hydrotechnical structure indicated in that provision. The Appendix to the C.L.A. describes hydrotechnical structures as:

- Category XXI construction objects—works related to water transport, such as: ports, harbours, artificial islands, basins, docks, breakwaters, quays, piers, jetties and slipways;
- Category XXVII construction objects—damming, overtopping and regulating structures, such as: dams, weirs, floodgates, sluices, siphons, dykes, canals, navigation locks, coastal bands and spurs and drainage ditches.

We should point out that all the above-mentioned structures which may constitute hydrotechnical structures are characterised by their stability and location in a particular place. The floating FSRU lacks these characteristics and, therefore, does not constitute a structure. This position is also supported by administrative courts' rulings issued about similar factual states. For example, we mention a judgement concerning the lack of real estate taxation on an object (a set of auxiliary pontoons that function

[12] https://www.marineinsight.com/types-of-ships/what-is-floating-storage-regasification-unit-fsru/, retrieved 23 May 2022.

[13] Judgement of the Supreme Administrative Court of 21 November 2019, II FSK 3861/17.

as a floating platform) registered in the administrative register of Polish inland navigation vessels; this object is characterised by mobility and, thus, constitutes 'movable property'.[14]

A separate issue is the possible taxation of the FSRU's equipment, particularly including its regasification installation. Regarding the consideration of treating this equipment as an element of the gas network, the same arguments should be cited as in the case of the onshore LNG terminal. The gas network can function without the regasification installation's connection to the network, so the installation cannot be regarded as an element of the construction object, ensuring the use of the structure for its intended purpose. Moreover, the FSRU's equipment cannot be regarded as a construction device either, since—according to the definition in Article 3(9) of the C.L.A.—a 'construction device' is technical equipment connected to a construction object that ensures its use for its intended purpose. However, as we have indicated, the FSRU does not constitute a construction object; consequently, the related equipment cannot be considered a construction device.

Our analysis in this subsection leads us to conclude that although the LNG onshore terminal and the FSRU have identical functions (the off-take of liquefied gas from tankers, its regasification and injection into the gas network), due to their different constructions, they present diametrically different cases from the real estate tax perspective. An onshore LNG terminal, as indicated above in Sect. 4.2.1, generates a very high tax burden because a significant part of its value is attributable to its structures' being subject to the real estate tax. At the other extreme is the FSRU, which—as a floating vessel—is not a construction object at all and, therefore, cannot be subject to the real estate tax. (Of course, the land portion of the investment, located outside the FSRU itself, will be subject to taxation, particularly the pipelines that will bring gas to the gas network).

4.3 Oil and Gas Tanks

The subject of taxation for various types of tanks has been among the most controversial topics in recent decade. This controversy is due to the L.T.C.A. definitions of taxable objects ('buildings' and 'structures'), which—in the case of certain categories of objects—may lead to unclear or difficult-to-accept conclusions. Of course, this difficulty would contribute only to academic discussions if not for the fact that buildings and structures have differently determined tax bases (buildings' usable areas versus structures' initial values). In many cases, classifying a given facility into one of these two categories results in a radically different tax charge. This problem is particularly visible in tanks' case.

Pursuant to the definition included in Article 1(a), Sect. 1.2, of the L.T.C.A., 'a structure' particularly denotes a construction object within the meaning of the provisions of the construction law which is neither a building nor a small architectural

[14] Judgement of the Provincial Administrative Court in Wrocław of 20 May 2021, I SA/Wr 690/20.

object. As we have already explained, the generally accepted and jurisprudentially confirmed (including in the judgements of the Constitutional Tribunal) method of interpreting this provision refers to the definition of a 'structure' from the C.L.A., which is indirectly indicated by the reference to the definition of a 'construction object' within the definition of a 'structure' in the Article 1a(1)(2) of the L.T.C.A. At the same time, the definition of a 'structure' in Article 3(3) of the C.L.A. indicates that a structure is any construction object which is neither a building nor a small architecture object. Significantly, the C.L.A'.s definition of a 'structure', in listing examples, does not indicate their constructional features but their functions (airports, sewage treatment plants, advertising facilities, tanks etc.). The construction method does not determine whether a given object is assigned to a given category but, rather, how it is used.

A reading of the definition of a 'structure' shows that, in order to determine whether an object can be classified as a structure, that it is not a building must first be determined. This requirement follows directly from the provision in both the L.T.C.A. and C.L.A. definitions of a 'structure'. (Article 1a(1)(2) L.T.C.A, Article 3(3) of the C.L.A.)

Pursuant to the definition of a 'building' set out in Article 1a(1)(1) of the L.T.C.A., building is a construction object within the meaning of the provisions of the construction law that is permanently connected to the ground, separated from space by means of building partitions and possessing foundations and a roof. Thus, in contrast to the definition of a 'structure' in the C.L.A., this definition of a 'building' does not refer to the object's function or purpose but only to its strictly defined structural features.

We should point out that many tanks which are construction objects meet the tax definition of a 'building' because they are separated from space by building partitions, have a roof and—due to their large size—foundations and are permanently connected to the ground. These conditions particularly apply not only to large silos for cement, sugar and grain but also to oil and gas tanks. Theoretically, from the perspective of the L.T.C.A. regulations' wording, such facilities should be taxed as buildings on their usable area because they cannot be qualified as 'structures' since they meet the definition of a 'building'. Nevertheless, this qualification has met with great resistance in practice from the tax authorities, as well as many administrative court judgements as described below. Before we discuss their positions on the regulations' interpretation, let us consider the reason for the disputes in the face of the regulations' seemingly clear construction.

The first reason is financial. Although large silos have relatively large surface areas (sometimes in the thousands of square metres), they are also very expensive structures. As a result, taxing them as buildings (based on their usable area) almost always entails a many-times-lower tax burden than if they were treated as structures (and taxed based on their initial value). The second and, apparently, key cause of disputes over tanks' tax qualification is semantics. Many objects (including tanks) which possess all the characteristics of buildings that we have mentioned (and, thus, should be treated as buildings, according to the tax provision) are not associated with buildings. Since these objects are not intended for inhabitation or use as work sites (like a 'building' in the commonly accepted sense of the term), they are often wrongly qualified as structures. According to this argument, although tanks possess the structural features of buildings, they should constitute structures due to their function.

The Constitutional Tribunal attempted to solve this problem in its judgement of 13 December 2017,[15] stating that a building object that fulfils all four prerequisites indicated in the definition of a 'building' cannot be regarded as a structure. At the same time, the Constitutional Tribunal indicated that certain objects with the characteristics of a building may be recognised by the legislator as structures in a special provision. The administrative courts subsequently referred to this fragment of the Constitutional Tribunal judgement's justification by issuing a number of judgements in 2018–2020 qualifying silos—which possess all the features of buildings—as structures. In the courts' opinion, the special provision (referred to by the Constitutional Tribunal) allowing a silo to be considered a structure is Article 3(3) of the C.L.A.; in its definition of a 'structure', this article lists tanks among other examples.[16] At the same time, the jurisprudence has also presented the opposite view, according to which the function or purpose of an object with the structural features of a building cannot change its tax qualification.[17]

Finally, given the divergent jurisprudence, one panel of judges presented the following legal issue for consideration by the Supreme Administrative Court through a resolution:

> Whether a construction object, which is a structure within the meaning of Article 3(3) C.L.A. in conjunction with Article 1a(1)(2) L.T.C.A. may be regarded for the purposes of real estate tax as a building within the meaning of Article 1a(1)(1) of the L.T.C.A.?[18]

The resolution of the panel of seven Supreme Administrative Court judges issued in response did not resolve the issue unequivocally. In accordance with the resolution, a construction object—which is a structure within the meaning of Article 3(3) of the C.L.A. in conjunction with Article 1a(1)(2) of the L.T.C.A.—may be deemed a building for the purposes of the real estate tax if it satisfies the criteria for a building set out in this provision and if its distinguishing feature is its usable area. This linking of the definition of a 'taxable object' with the provision regulating the taxable base has been criticised by representatives of the doctrine (Etel, 2022, pp. 6–11). At the same time, the criterion of a 'usable area' may, in practice, help resolve qualification disputes; however, the objective criteria on which taxpayers and tax authorities will be able to determine whether a given object has a distinguishing feature in the form of usable area are unclear (Kałążny, 2022, pp. 32–36).

In concluding our discussion of oil and gas tanks' tax treatment, we should point out that this issue sparks serious controversies and has not been unambiguously resolved in the jurisprudence. The classification of tanks as 'structures', which is

[15] SK 48/15.

[16] This provision is referred to, for example, in the Supreme Administrative Court judgement of 8 May 2018, II FSK 1281/16.

[17] Judgement of the Supreme Administrative Court of 16 March 2021, III FSK 3294/21.

[18] Judgement of the Supreme Administrative Court of 13 July 2021, III FSK 1611/21.

most frequently accepted in practice, is associated with significantly higher real estate taxes than if they were classified as buildings and, it seems, is not always consistent with regulations. (However, at the same time, it is consistent with the common understanding of the notions of a 'building' and a 'structure').

Chapter 5
The Taxation of Construction Objects Used to Generate Energy: The Current Legal Regime

Abstract The interrelation between the real estate tax and the construction law makes a facility's structural aspects crucial for taxation. With similar investment outlays, two plants may generate different tax amounts if one of them comprises mainly single-storey buildings filled with equipment while the other contains a significant amount of equipment with construction parts or large tanks. This specificity in Polish tax rules is very well illustrated by the taxation of various types of power plants. The amount of tax is not always determined directly by the cost of a given facility's construction or, for example, its installed electric power but by the structural specifics of a given type of power plant. Coal-fired power plants are in a privileged position, with a relatively small proportion of the inputs qualifying to be taxed as structures. The total cost of energy production, in their case, also includes the tax to be paid by the coal mine. The cost of the tax on the source of the energy raw material is, of course, not present in the case of renewable energy. At the same time, due to their structural specificity (few buildings), a potentially large part of the outlays could be subject to a high tax as a structure (2% of their value per year). However, this circumstance is mitigated by the legislator and the jurisprudence, which allow for the most valuable elements of the installation (turbines at wind power plants and panels at photovoltaic plants) to be excluded from the scope of taxation. Quite unexpectedly—and, seemingly, accidentally—biogas plants, in which tanks play an important role, are disadvantaged in terms of taxation. Taxing tanks as structures significantly increases the amount of tax paid on such power plants, and attempts to change this state of affairs through interpretation have, so far, not succeeded.

Keywords Coal-fired power plants · Gas-fired power plants · Oil power plants · Wind power plants · Hydroelectric power stations · Geothermal power plants · Photovoltaic power plants · Biogas plants · Waste incineration plants with thermal energy recovery · Nuclear power plants

W. Morawski and A. Kałążny, *The Taxation of Energy-Sector Assets: Polish Tax Legislation on the Eve of Energy Transformation*, SpringerBriefs in Energy,
https://doi.org/10.1007/978-3-031-15673-1_5

5.1 Coal-Fired Power Plants

The administrative courts' jurisprudence on the taxation of coal-fired power plants has been relatively stable. As a rule, equipment used to generate electricity is located in buildings, so they are not taxed separately as structures (tax is calculated on the building's usable area, while the equipment's value is beyond the scope of taxation) (Morawski, 2014, pp. 103–110). This solution is very favourable for entrepreneurs. Such a qualification is based on the assumption that the foundation or construction part of a technical device located in a building is a construction part of that building; therefore, it does not constitute a separate construction object. At the same time, in order to classify a given object (in this case, the foundation of technical equipment) as a 'structure', it must be proved to constitute an autonomous construction object which is separate from the building.

The definition of a 'structure' in Article 3(3) of the C.L.A. lists exemplary technical facilities with a construction part that constitutes a structure. It does not entirely clarify what the legislator's intention was in adding to the open definition (it only lists exemplary structures) another, semi-open catalogue of technical facilities with construction parts while simultaneously indicating that it also includes 'other equipments'. Seemingly, the purpose of indicating specific instances of equipment in this provision of the construction law may have been the tax context. This purpose was certain in the case of wind power plants and nuclear power plants, so boilers can be assumed to have been included in this provision for a similar reason. For the devices mentioned by name, doubtless, only their construction parts constitute a structure (and, thus, the subject of taxation), while the equipment itself is not subject to taxation.

At the same time, we should point out that the administrative courts have, in some rulings, accepted the taxation of structures in buildings—mainly when concerning the taxation of the construction parts (foundations) of turbines, boilers et cetera as structures.[1] The argument in favour of taxing such structures derives from the fact that technical equipment with a very large mass (such as turbines or boilers in power plants), requires foundations independent from a building and not technically connected to its structure. Such a foundation, despite its location inside a building, indeed constitutes a construction object separate from the building in the form of a structure. Notably, even when taxing foundations located inside a building, technical equipment itself remains beyond the scope of taxation.

The greatest number of problems regarding interpretation of tax definitions have concerned the taxation of environmental protection equipment. The taxation of electrostatic precipitators and flue gas desulphurisation installations has been subjected to numerous, often changing decisions by administrative courts. For many years, the courts have ruled that an entire facility—including both the construction parts and the technical equipment used for flue gas cleaning—is subject to taxation.[2] Only in a

[1] Judgement of the Provincial Administrative Court in Gliwice of 20.07.2010, I SA/Gl 424/10.

[2] E.g., the judgements of the Provincial Administrative Court in Gliwice of 7 July 2008, I SA/Gl 48/08, I SA/Gl 49/08, I SA/Gl 50/08, I SA/Gl 51/08 and I SA/Gl 52/08; the judgements of the

few rulings has the court allowed for the possibility of taxing an electrostatic precipitator facility as a building,[3] which was the most favourable from the tax perspective, because such a building has relatively small usable area (taxable base) and the value of the facility in such case is not a subject to tax.[4] In recent years, following the change in the definition of a 'construction object' on 28 June 2015 (Act on 20.02.2015 on change of CLA Journal of Laws 2015, item 443), when the passages indicating a structure as a technical and utilitarian whole disappeared, the administrative courts have held that only objects' construction parts, such as electrostatic precipitators, are taxable.[5] Nevertheless, we should point out too few judgements favourable to taxpayers have been able to speak of an established line of jurisprudence that would exclude the value of electrostatic precipitator devices from taxation.

In the case of coal-fired power generation, land taxation is scarcely relevant. The land on which such power plants are located is subject to the real estate tax at the maximum rate, like any land related to economic activity. However, this burden is not particularly onerous—it is typical for a business entity.

The situation differs for lignite power plants, which are closely linked to existing lignite mines in their vicinity (due to the unprofitable transport of lignite). A lignite mine occupies a fairly large area of land, which is taxed at the highest real estate tax rates since it is associated with and occupied for business activities. (For more on the taxation of lignite mine land, see Chap. 7: The Taxation of Land Used for Energy Production).

5.2 Gas-Fired Power Plants

The specificity of taxing gas-fired power stations is related to the energy production technology they use. A gas power plant, based on clean fuel and modern technology, does not emit as many pollutants as coal power plants (as a result of natural gas combustion, no harmful sulphur oxides are produced, while the nitrogen oxides and carbon dioxide content is reduced by half compared to coal combustion). For this reason, gas power plants do not require as many environmental protection devices, which limits the problem concerning their potential taxation as structures. An as indirect result, a gas-fired power station is smaller, which is reflected in its buildings' less extensive usable area.

Supreme Administrative Court of 7 July 2009, II FSK 2093/08, II FSK 2094/08, II FSK 2095/08 and II FSK 2096/08, and the judgements of the Provincial Administrative Court in Gdańsk of 7 September 2011, I SA/Gd 442/11, I SA/Gd 443/11, I SA/Gd 444/11, I SA/Gd 445/11, I SA/Gd 446/11, I SA/Gd 447/11, I SA/Gd 448/11, I SA/Gd 449/11 and I SA/Gd 450/11, as confirmed by the judgements of the Supreme Administrative Court of 19 April 2013, II FSK 3005/11, II FSK 3006/11, II FSK 3007/11, II FSK 3008/11, II FSK 3009/11, II FSK 3010/11 and II FSK 3011/11.

[3] The Provincial Administrative Court in Gliwice in the judgement of 25 April 2012, I SA/Gl 1069/11.

[4] This decision was due to their small footprint and the low tax rates on buildings.

[5] Judgement of the Supreme Administrative Court of 31.01.2019, II FSK 123/17.

In principle, a gas-fired power station also does not require tanks for its raw material (gas) since it is supplied directly by a pipeline. Compared to coal-fired power stations, which require space for fuel storage and waste storage, a gas-fired power station—therefore—takes up less space, resulting in less land tax.

5.3 Oil Power Plants

Oil power plants are rarely used in Poland. (As of 2022, only two power plants of this type operate in the country, using oil as an energy raw material for energy production).[6] In principle, some of the tax problems facing both coal power plants (expensive environmental equipment) and gas power plants (small area, and a lack of storage yards for raw material and waste) also affect this type of power plant.

A specific feature of oil power plants is their oil tanks. They are relatively large, highly valuable objects. Taxing them as structures would entail a high tax burden. Meanwhile, in recent few years, a discussion in Poland has disputed large tanks' tax classification. (For more on this topic, see Sect. 4.3: 'Oil and Gas Storage Tanks'). The possible taxation of oil tanks as buildings (on the basis of their usable area) would entail a significantly lower tax burden (versus taxing them as structures). Nevertheless, administrative courts' current approach to taxing this type of facility is rather unfavourable to taxpayers (see Sect. 4.3.).

5.4 Wind Power Plants

In the current legal framework, the taxation of wind *power* plants does not provoke any major uncertainties; however, in last five years, it was subjected to numerous, radical legislative changes (for more detail, see Chap. 6: 'The Taxation of Wind Power Plants: A Case of Regulatory Instability'). The construction part of a wind power plant—that is, its foundation and tower—is subject to taxation (as a structure). On the other hand, the technical equipment installed on the tower that generates electricity is beyond the scope of taxation. Therefore, most of a wind power plant's expenditures are not included in the real estate tax base.

Since the amendment of the regulations in 2018,[7] uncertainties beyond the tax qualification of the wind power plant itself have related to the taxation of the accompanying infrastructure—particularly the power equipment and the buildings included in transformer stations. (For more on this topic, see Sect. 10.2: 'Transformer Stations'.)

Land taxation is not a major issue for wind turbines since they cover a small area. Particular problems are related to the taxation of offshore wind farms located outside Poland's territorial sea but in the Polish Exclusive Economic Zone. (For more on this

[6] https://pl.wikipedia.org/wiki/Lista_elektrowni_w_Polsce retrieved 23 May 2022.
[7] Journal of Laws of 2018, item 1276.

topic, see Chap. 8: 'Offshore Wind Farms: Special Rules on the Taxation of Specific Assets'.)

5.5 Hydroelectric Power Stations

The most important part of a hydroelectric power plant is the hydrotechnical structures used to produce electricity. The definition of a 'structure' in Article 3(3) of the C.L.A. points directly to hydrotechnical structures as an example of a structure; therefore, they should be subject to the real estate tax. Notably, a hydroelectric power plant—apart from its hydrotechnical structures—also includes technical equipment, such as turbines. Given the courts' current views on the taxation of other technical equipment (especially after the amendment to the construction law, which was entered into force on 28 June 2015)[8], only the construction parts of such equipment (perhaps particularly the aforementioned hydrotechnical structures) should be assumed to be subject to taxation. Meanwhile, the technical equipment itself lies beyond the scope of taxation.

An analysis of the Polish administrative courts' jurisprudence leads to the conclusion that the specific ownership of hydroelectric power plants may lead to a different tax treatment than other types of power plants. In the judgement of 11 January 2018,[9] the Supreme Administrative Court concluded that a hydroelectric power plant is not a construct related to conducting economic activity. This ruling was due to the fact that the power plant in question was under the control of the Regional Water Management Board (RZGW). In terms of Polish law, the RZGW is a budgetary unit whose main purpose is not to conduct business activity. In such a case, the structures comprising the power plant would not be subject to the real estate tax because only structures related to conducting business activity are subject to taxation. However, this position is very controversial because the RZGW sells the energy generated by the power plant; therefore, although this operation does not constitute a typical enterprise, the RZGW undertakes an activity which constitutes organised profit-making, conducted continuously and on its own behalf.[10] The reasoning presented by the court led to privileging entities which are organisational units of the State Treasury over entrepreneurs conducting similar activities.

An important issue for hydroelectric power plants is land taxation. Hydroelectric power plants are sometimes associated with vast areas of undeveloped land. According to the regulations (Article 2(2) and 7(10) of the L.T.C.A.), if such land is classified as 'agricultural land' or 'wasteland', it should be subject to the real estate tax only for the areas that are occupied for business activity. The jurisprudence indicates that the land used by a hydroelectric power plant, should be treated as land

---

[8] Journal of Laws 2015, item 443.

[9] II FSK 3373/15.

[10] Article 3 of the Business Law.

occupied for business activity.[11] At the same time, the courts emphasise that whenever a specific part of a plot of land must be designated as floodplain or protection zone, the remaining part of the plot should not be treated as occupied for economic activity and, consequently, should not be subject to the real estate tax.[12]

5.6 Geothermal Power Plants

Boreholes are the most important element of a geothermal power plant from the perspective of real estate taxation. 'Boreholes' should be defined as a type of excavation· Excavation (in hard coal mines) has been subjected to a number of disputes, ending (to some extent) with a judgement of the Constitutional Tribunal of 13 September 2011.[13] (For more on this topic, see Chap. 3: 'The Taxation of Assets Used to Extract Energy Resources'.) Pursuant to the conclusion of this judgement (which is generally accepted by the administrative courts[14]), *underground excavation*—understood as a space underground—does not constitute structures subject to the real estate tax; however, the objects located in this space may be subject to taxation if they are structures.

The guidelines contained in the Constitutional Tribunal judgement concerning a coal mine are not easy to apply to a very specific excavation, such as a geothermal borehole. In principle, the cost of drilling should not itself be included in the real estate tax base (just as the cost of excavating a pit for a mine is not included). However, facilities located at a borehole may be taxed as structures, provided that they are assigned to one of the categories explicitly listed in the definition of 'structures' in Article 3(3) of the C.L.A. For mines, a typically taxable element of an excavation is mining supports, classified as a 'retaining structure' and listed as 'structures' in Article 3(3) of the C.L.A. In the case of boreholes, special pipes perform this function.

As the Provincial Administrative Court in Szczecin noted in its judgement of 7 October 2015,[15] the taxable structures within a geothermal borehole are the casing with its Johnson filter, the fittings and the wellhead. While the piping, as a linear object, is included in the C.L.A. regulations as an example structure, the filter or the wellhead are, rather, technical devices—the taxation of which through the real estate tax must be questioned.[16]

A geothermal power plant also includes above-ground infrastructure, comprising the technical equipment necessary for the energy production process (expanders,

---

[11] Judgement of the Provincial Administrative Court in Szczecin of 22 May 2019, I SA/Sz 183/19.

[12] Ibidem.

[13] P 33/09.

[14] Judgement of the Supreme Administrative Court of 20 April 2022, III FSK 456/21.

[15] I SA/Sz 907/15.

[16] This ambiguity was pointed out by the Provincial Administrative Court in Bydgoszcz in its judgement of 22 January 2019, I SA/Bd 938/18. However, this judgement concerned more complicated gas boreholes.

condensers and turbines), their construction parts (the foundations or buildings upon or in which they are located) and pipelines. The taxation of such assets does not fundamentally differ from the taxation of equipment and construction parts operating in other types of power plants.

Land taxation does not play a significant role for geothermal power plants because they do not occupy a significant area at the ground level and their underground portion is not taxable (as land).

5.7 Photovoltaic Power Plants

The main tax problem concerning photovoltaic power plants is the question of where the construction part of the technical equipment (the taxable structure) ends and where the technical equipment itself (the object beyond the scope of taxation) begins. Therefore, the issue of their taxation is similar to wind power plants' case, except that—contrary to wind power plants—a photovoltaic power plant is not explicitly mentioned in the C.L.A. definition of a 'structure' as an example of technical equipment, the construction part of which constitutes a structure. However, this lack of a literal mention of a photovoltaic power plant in the aforementioned provision bears no significance for such plants' tax treatment since the catalogue of technical equipment with construction parts listed in Article 3(3) of the C.L.A. serves only as non-exhaustive examples. This position was confirmed by the Supreme Administrative Court in its judgement of 22 October 2018,[17] in which it indicated that the deletion of 'wind power plant' from Article 3(3) of the C.L.A. should not affect the real estate tax treatment of a wind power plant.

Photovoltaic panels are typically mounted on support structures that form photovoltaic farms or on the roofs of buildings, providing a source of electricity. Each of these cases gives rise to slightly different tax consequences.

Photovoltaic farms placed directly on the ground are built of photovoltaic panels which are attached to metal tables. In turn, these tables are bolted down, usually to a metal support structure, part of which is driven into the ground (usually using a special pile driver) to ensure the entire structure's stability. All such farms' solar panels are connected by a set of cables to electrical equipment, such as generators and transformer stations, allowing the circulation of energy generated by the photovoltaic panels.

Regarding such on-the-ground photovoltaic farms, the jurisprudence and doctrine have presented the position that all the elements of a photovoltaic farm (including solar panels), as a power grid forming a technical and utilitarian whole, constitute a taxable structure (Pahl, 2014).[18] This position is, obviously, disadvantageous for

[17] II FSK 2983/17.

[18] Judgement of the Provincial Administrative Court in Szczecin of 6 December 2017, I SA/Sz 760/17, overruled by the judgement of the Supreme Administrative Court of 18 December 2018, II FSK 1275/18.

taxpayers because it results in including most (if not all) expenditures for the construction of such a power plant in the tax base. In recent years, a much more favourable position for taxpayers has begun to prevail in the jurisprudence. As the courts have indicated, due to the differences between, on the one hand, the construction of solar panels and support elements and, on the other hand, the function performed by these elements,[19] photovoltaic panels should be treated as technical equipment, and only their construction part (in the form of a system for fixing panels) should be taxed as a structure.[20] Thus, according to this approach, photovoltaic panels on support elements are treated as the technical equipment listed in the definition of a 'structure' in Article 3(3) of C.L.A., which have a construction part in the form of a support element.

Neither jurisprudence nor regulations explicitly indicate what should be considered a 'construction part' of a photovoltaic farm. The mounting system for solar panels—so-called support elements—usually comprises several elements that are more or less similar in terms of their technical parameters, not all of which are driven into the ground. Different descriptions of photovoltaic farm structures can be found in the jurisprudence. They are indicated as 'structural tables on which panels (photovoltaic cells) are mounted, attached to poles driven into the ground'.[21] Other judgements refer, rather, to 'panels (photovoltaic cells) fixed to the ground by a special system of anchors, piling or by concrete slabs'.[22] This constructional diversity causes uncertainty as to whether, for example, the panels' easily dismantled fastening elements should also qualify as a 'construction part' of a photovoltaic farm. Seemingly, support elements that are permanently connected with the ground—which determine the stability of the entire facility and, at the same time, cannot be replaced without damage (Kałążny& Jankowska, 2022, pp. 39–45)—should be regarded as construction parts.

Photovoltaic panels mounted on the roofs of buildings are a separate issue. As a rule, they are not power plants in the strict sense, although they generate electricity and feed it into the power grid. Therefore, it seems that such distributed energy sources should also be considered as part of the power grid. The jurisprudence indicates that photovoltaic panels installed on the roof of a building should be treated as technical devices that can be taxed, at most, on the construction part (if they have such a part).[23] Panels on the roof of a building, obviously, do not have a support element driven into the ground. Their construction part is the building on which they are placed

---

[19] Photovoltaic panels, usually made of silicon, convert solar energy into electricity. Meanwhile, usually, metal support structures serve as a kind of scaffolding, ensuring—inter alia—a stable foundation for the entire facility on the ground.

[20] See judgement of the Supreme Administrative Court of 18 December 2018, II FSK 1275/18; judgement of the Provincial Administrative Court judgement in Szczecin of 11 September 2019, I SA/Sz 239/19; judgement of the Provincial Administrative Court in Szczecin of 9 January 2014, I SA/Sz 854/13.

[21] Judgement of the Supreme Administrative Court of 18 December 2018, II FSK 1275/18.

[22] Judgement of the Provincial Administrative Court in Szczecin of 9 January 2014, I SA/Sz 854/13; judgement of the Provincial Administrative Court in Opole of 13 June 2014, I SA/Op 327/14.

[23] Judgement of the Provincial Administrative Court in Warsaw of 7.01.2021, III SA/Wa 1334/20.

(which is taxed on its usable area). Alternatively, photovoltaic panels on the roof of a building may be assumed not to have a construction part subject to real estate tax at all (while they are not a freestanding technical device indicated in the definition of a 'structure' in Article 3[3] of the C.L.A. because they are located on the roof of a building). The qualification of panels on roofs has not been unambiguously resolved in the jurisprudence of administrative courts due to the few judgements that have addressed this issue. Notably, in their judgements, the courts have rejected the concept of treating a photovoltaic panel on the roof of a building as construction device connected with the construction object that ensures the possibility of using the object in accordance with its purpose (which, in accordance with the L.T.C.A. definition of a 'structure', would require treating the panel as a taxed object).[24]

In the case of photovoltaic power plants, an important real estate tax issue is the taxation of land, due to the large area of land that such plants occupy. (For more on this issue, see Chap. 7: 'The Taxation of Land Used for Energy Production'.)

5.8 Biogas Plants

One specific element of biogas plants that distinguishes them from other types of power plants is the tanks they use to produce gas. Although various types of tanks can also be found in other types of power plants, for biogas plants, tanks' cost constitutes a significant part of the entire plant's expenditure, so the tanks' tax classification significantly affects the total tax burden of the entire biogas plant. Fundamentally, this issue concerns whether biogas plant tanks are buildings or structures. The tax classification of tanks with the features of buildings has been subjected to discussion in Poland in recent years. A resolution to this matter was attempted by the Constitutional Tribunal in its judgement of 13 December 2017.[25] This judgement indicates that, if an object fulfils the premises indicated in the definition of a 'building', it can no longer be a structure. However, the tribunal's judgement did not influence administrative courts' jurisprudence, which consistently ordered that objects performing the function of a reservoir should be qualified as structures—even if they meet the definition of a 'building' (Article 3(3) of the C.L.A.). This position was also presented in judgements concerning biogas plants' tanks, which are treated as structures.[26] Therefore, their value—and not their usable area—is subject to taxation. The latest development in this discussion is the resolution of the panel of seven judges of the Supreme Administrative Court on 29 September 2021.[27] When qualifying 'tanks', this panel ordered the analysis of an additional premise not indicated in the L.T.C.A. regulations: the possession of a distinguishing feature in the form of usable area. (For more on this topic, see Chap. 4: 'The Taxation of Assets Used to Transport and Store

[24] Judgement of the Provincial Administrative Court in Warsaw of 7.01.2021. III SA/Wa 1334/20.
[25] SK 48/15.
[26] Judgement of the Supreme Administrative Court of 7 November 2019, II FSK 1244/19.
[27] III FPS 1/21.

Energy Resources'). The aforementioned resolution's effects on the tax treatment of biogas plant tanks is difficult to unequivocally determine. Seemingly, in the cases of many biogas plant tanks, this usable area can be determined, which offers taxpayers potential hope for more favourable tax treatment.

Another feature specific to biogas plants is that they are often linked to the agricultural sector. Taxpayers have taken the position that biogas plants are connected precisely with agricultural activity and not business activity, since they produce electricity for the exclusive use of agricultural entities. Such a qualification means primarily that the structure is not subject to real estate tax; however, the administrative courts did not agree with this argument.[28]

5.9 Waste Incineration Plants with Thermal Energy Recovery

Waste incineration plants are, as a rule, designed to comprise buildings with a large volume which house the technical equipment needed for both waste incineration and the generation of heat and electricity. For this reason, they do not stand out from a tax perspective compared to coal-fired power plants—although they are, obviously, smaller plants.

As with coal-fired power plants, the most important tax issue facing such incineration plants is the tax treatment of technical equipment located inside their buildings. Generally, they should not be treated as taxable structures, though in some cases, their foundations may be taxed even if they are located fully within a building. (For more on this topic, see Sect. 5.1: 'Coal-Fired Power Plants').

5.10 Nuclear Power Plants

Poland has no nuclear power plants, but preparatory work has begun with varying intensity for several decades. One manifestation of these preparations is the shaping of current legislation designed for future nuclear installations. Particularly, legislators decided to unequivocally protect potential investors from an entire nuclear installation's being taxed as a structure, which could reduce such a project's overall profitability. For this reason, they decided to clarify the definition of a 'structure' in Article 3.3 of the C.L.A. By virtue of the act of 29 June 2011 on the preparation and realisation of investments in nuclear power facilities and accompanying investments, the term 'nuclear power plants, as well as the construction parts of technical equipment (boilers, industrial furnaces, wind power plants and other equipments)' appeared in part of the definition. This change should be described as apparent

[28] Judgement of the Provincial Administrative Court in Gdansk of 26 November 2019, I SA/Gd 1378/19.

since the phrase 'and other equipments' would still apply to a nuclear power plant. However, since a similar 'manoeuvre' in the case of wind power plants (adding the words 'wind power plants') solved the taxation of technical device problem in taxpayers' favour (see Sect. 5.6), perhaps also in the case of nuclear power plants, legislators were hoping for a similar effect. Moreover, much of nuclear power plants' valuable technical equipment is kept in their buildings, so only the buildings would be taxed, not the equipment inside.

Interestingly, regulations on preparing nuclear power plant investments also introduced (for the first time in Poland) a mechanism for distributing real estate tax revenue between municipalities. Legislators assumed, based on the current legal framework, that a nuclear power plant would generate gigantic revenues in one municipality while also generating costs in neighbouring municipalities (e.g., related to the construction of transport infrastructure and its maintenance). Moreover, the proximity of a nuclear power plant may also negatively affect, for instance, tourism revenues—not only in the municipality where it is located but also in a number of surrounding municipalities. According to the introduced provision, the real estate tax will formally constitute income for the municipality where the nuclear power plant is located; therefore, this municipality will levy and collect the tax. However, the municipality on whose territory the nuclear power plant, or part of it, is located will be obliged to pay the neighbouring municipalities a fee equal to 50% of the real estate tax paid on the power plant.[29] This fee will be divided in equal parts between all municipalities bordering the municipality where the nuclear power plant is wholly or partially located.[30] This solution may raise some doubts. First, the impact of a nuclear power plant may extend beyond the municipalities that directly neighbour the municipality where the plant is located. Second, why a similar mechanism was not introduced for other facilities that generate very large tax revenues, such as coal-fired power plants or the onshore LNG terminal, is puzzling. It is, however, a valuable progress and one can only hope that this solution will be further developed and applied on a wider scale.

---

[29] Article 50(1) of the Act of 29 June 2011 (on the preparation and implementation of investments in nuclear power facilities and accompanying investments).

[30] Article 50(2) of the Act of 29 June 2011.

Chapter 6
The Taxation of Wind Power Plants: A Case of Regulatory Instability

Abstract Changes to the regulations governing the taxation of wind farms in Poland are a difficult-to-understand example of legislators' irrationality. The uncontrolled construction of wind farms anywhere should, obviously, not be accepted because they can be a nuisance to local residents. However, the approaches so far to this problem can be described only as absurd. That the tax regulations which have undermined many wind power plants' functioning were introduced accidentally is particularly sad. The jurisprudence of administrative courts is also difficult to assess positively. They have, de facto, accepted the low quality of tax law in Poland. Of course, one can understand that judges tried to shape wind power investments regulations rationally. However, one cannot accept a line of reasoning suggesting that, since an intertemporal provision has been applied, the content of the legal regulation has changed. The analysed legal regulation was simply so defective that it should be assessed by the Constitutional Tribunal. Fortunately, Polish legislators are gradually withdrawing from the solutions adopted in 2016.

Keywords Wind farm · Real estate tax · Instability of the law

6.1 Wind Power Plants: Introduction

A wind power plant primarily comprises wind turbines (when it includes more than one turbine, it is called a 'wind farm'). Turbines may be of various designs, and they are generally divided into *vertical axis turbines* and *propeller turbines with a horizontal axis of rotation*. Their design does not affect their taxation rules.

The main component of a wind turbine is the turbine itself, which comprises a tower set on a foundation and a nacelle that houses the generator and other equipment to ensure energy production. The turbine is connected to the electricity grid via a connection. Additionally, a wind turbine may include such facilities as fencing or

The chapter is, inter alia, the result of research carried out under the grant funded by the National Science Centre (Poland) No. 2019/35/B/HS5/00554, 'Interpretation of tax law in the context of passing time'.

W. Morawski and A. Kałążny, *The Taxation of Energy-Sector Assets: Polish Tax Legislation on the Eve of Energy Transformation*, SpringerBriefs in Energy,
https://doi.org/10.1007/978-3-031-15673-1_6

access roads. The most common wind turbine in Poland is a three-bladed propeller turbine with a horizontal axis of rotation.

The problem of taxing wind power plants in Poland resembles a dynamic action film in which the situation is constantly changing and the main character often stares into the eyes of death only to finally reach a happy ending (Morawski & Kałążny, 2021, p. 8). But even so, not everyone will be happy.

6.2 Taxed in Full?

Wind energy has developed in Poland over the last decade or so. For various reasons, it was long a mere curiosity and not a significant element of the Polish energy sector. One barrier to this sector's development was the unfavourable real estate tax regime for wind farms. Court rulings were dominated by a concept unfavourable for taxpayers, according to which entire wind power plants were taxed as structures.[1] The courts held that a wind power plant must be considered a functional whole and, therefore, taxed as a whole. Naturally, the administrative courts then pointed to the reference in the definition of a 'structure' in Article 3(3)(b) of the C.L.A. to a structure as a technical and functional whole.

6.3 Taxing Only the Construction Part?

Around 2009, the jurisprudence of Polish administrative courts gradually changed, becoming very favourable for entrepreneurs operating wind power plants.[2] This shift was part of an overall change in the Polish administrative courts' jurisprudential concepts related to the taxation of many types of industrial facilities. More and more often, the courts began to accept that only these facilities' construction parts should be taxed.[3]

However, fully connecting the changes in the jurisprudence concerning the rules of taxing wind power plants to analogous changes concerning other industrial facilities does not seem reasonable. For wind power plants, the administrative courts' jurisprudence indicated a specific reason for the change in views: a change in the law. This meant that, in relation to cases concerning periods before the change in the law, the old view of taxing the wind power plant in its entirety continued to apply.

---

[1] Among other judgements, see Judgement of the Provincial Administrative Court in Szczecin of 4 April 2006, I SA/Sz 882/04 (a dispute related to a tax assessment for 2004); judgement of the Provincial Administrative Court in Bydgoszcz of 23 March 2009, I SA/Bd 3/09 (the verdict was repealed by the Supreme Administrative Court verdict of 25 November 2010, II FSK 1382/09).

[2] Judgement of the Supreme Administrative Court of 30 July 2009, II FSK 202/08; judgement of the Supreme Administrative Court of 5 January 2010, II FSK 1101/08.

[3] See Sect. 2.4: 'The Real Estate Tax on Structures'.

The aforementioned amendment concerned the wording of Article 3(3) of the C.L.A. Until 28 July 2005, this provision stated that structures were 'also the construction parts of technical installations (boilers, industrial furnaces and other installations)'. After the amendment, the provision read as follows: 'also construction parts of technical equipment (boilers, industrial furnaces, wind power plants and other installations) and foundations for machinery and equipment, as technically separate parts of objects constituting a functional whole'. A comparison of the provision's content before and after the amendment leads to the obvious conclusion that this change was, at most, a *pseudo-amendment*. Simply put, even before this change, wind turbines should have been treated as 'technical installations' or 'other installations'. It also follows that before this change, wind power plants should have been taxed such that only their construction parts would have been subject to taxation. The apparent change has given the administrative courts an opportunity to retreat from an ill-considered line of jurisprudence. In any case, one may suspect that this opportunity was the legislators' intention.[4]

Without changes to the rules on the real estate taxation of wind power plants, these plants could not become profitable enough to encourage entrepreneurs to invest in wind energy. Legislators seemed concerned about unequivocally deciding that all technical facilities are taxable as construction parts, so they chose the path of 'resolving doubts' only in relation to wind power plants, where reducing the tax burden was simply necessary. This decision was also due to the fact that, at that time, the view that only the construction parts of coal-fired power plants were taxable was not questioned. Given, additionally, that coal-fired power plants are usually old facilities and, therefore, that their tax base was relatively low due to inflation, the change turns out to be fully rational in order to level the playing field between different energy sectors.

However, this change initiated a rather strange custom among the Polish legislators, who—depending on their needs—add or remove particular types of power plants from the content of 3(3) of the C.LA.

[4] Notably, the letter of the Department of Local Taxes and Fees of 17 May 2007, No. PL-833/35/07/ /IP/346 (Biuletyn Skarbowy 2007, 3, 21) stated that the entire wind power plant cannot be regarded as a structure but only its construction parts (such as foundations and towers) as technically separate parts of objects constituting a functional whole. As a result, such devices as rotors with blades, generators, gearboxes, control computers, transformers, electrical switchgears, alarm systems and remote control systems are neither structures nor construction devices within the meaning of the Construction Law. Rather, they only constitute 'technical and technological equipment of the power plant'. The change, therefore, seems to implement the Minister of Finance's concept, which for quite a long time was not accepted by municipalities' tax authorities. The Minister of Finance has quite limited opportunities to influence municipal tax authorities' jurisprudence practices.

6.4 The 'Anti-Windmill' Law

The dynamic development of wind energy in Poland was suddenly threatened by the Law of 20 May 2016 on wind power investments.[5] This law had aimed to tidy up the issues facing onshore wind energy investments; however, it contained solutions that, in practice, made building wind power plants on land almost impossible. Undoubtedly, the most dangerous aspect for new investments turned out to be the 10H rule, according to which wind turbines may not be built at a distance from buildings of less than 10 times the wind turbine's height. This provision meant that almost the entire Polish territory became inaccessible for wind energy investments. This impact already justified the law's being quite commonly referred to as the 'anti-windmill law' or comparing the government's efforts to Don Quixote's tilting against windmills. Of course, the spontaneous establishment of wind turbines without any restrictions, close to residential buildings, could no longer be accepted. Unfortunately, instead of rational restrictions that would protect the interests of residents, who until now could do nothing to oppose wind turbines near their homes, a de facto ban on the construction of new wind turbines was proposed.

While working on the act, initially, its authors did not realise that changes in the law would also have tax consequences. When, as soon as during the legislative process, doubts began to arise in this respect, an intertemporal provision was introduced under which the tax effects of the act were deferred. According to Article 17 of the W.P.P.A.: 'From the date of entry into force of the Act until 31.12.2016, real estate tax on wind power plants shall be determined and collected in accordance with the provisions in force before the date of entry into force of the Act'.

The W.P.P.A. did not amend the L.T.C.A. itself, but it did amend the C.L.A. The anti-windmill law itself defined a *wind power plant* as 'a structure within the meaning of the provisions of the construction law, consisting at least of a foundation, a tower and technical elements, with a capacity greater than the capacity of a micro-installation within the meaning of Article 2 (19) of the Act of 20 February 2015 on Renewable Energy Sources (Journal of Laws, item 478 and 2365)'.[6] Additionally, the W.P.P.A. changed the content of the enumeration of 'structures' contained in Article 3(3) of the C.L.A. by removing wind power plants. This change reversed the changes introduced on 28 June 2005—that is, wind turbines disappeared from the enumeration of technical facilities' construction parts.

However, these changes were introduced rather clumsily, so whether the rules on taxing wind power plants had really changed was not at all clear. For example, according to the judgement of the Constitutional Tribunal of 13 September 2011 (P 33/09), the condition for taxing a facility was its specification as a 'structure' in a provision of the act. Therefore, the act should provide that structures include, inter alia, entire wind power plants. Meanwhile, in the W.P.P.A., legislators stipulated only that a 'wind power plant' is an object with certain features, one of which is its being a structure. As a result, a linguistic interpretation of the provision could lead to the

[5] Journal of Laws 2016, item 961, hereinafter further to as the 'anti-windmill law' or 'W.P.P.A.'.

[6] Article 2(1), W.P.P.A.

conclusion that whether a typical wind power plant is a wind power plant within the meaning of the W.P.P.A. is not at all certain since its status as a structure is unknown.

These ambiguities triggered a wave of disputes in administrative courts. Rulings by provincial administrative courts were most often unfavourable to taxpayers; the courts held that the entire facility should be taxed (e.g. the Provincial Administrative Court in Bydgoszcz ruling of 21 February 2017[7]; the Provincial Administrative Court in Gorzów Wielkopolski ruling of 8 March 2017[8]; the Provincial Administrative Court in Olsztyn ruling of 23 March 2017[9]; the Provincial Administrative Court judgement in Rzeszów of 13 June 2017[10]). This assertion was accompanied by the courts' unequivocally expressed belief that the law had changed and that 'these changes result in an increase in the burden of taxation on this type of facilities'.[11] The problem had to be resolved by the Supreme Administrative Court, which issued a judgement by a panel of seven judges (it usually decides with a panel of three judges) on 22 October 2018,[12] when it ruled on whether the taxation of wind turbines had changed. The court ruled that a wind power plant as a whole—that is, including its technical parts—is taxable. The court's reasoning was based, inter alia, on the argument that since an intertemporal provision postpones the tax effects of a change in legal regulation, the change must have been real. In our view, this line of reasoning is at least questionable, especially given the manner in which the W.P.P.A. was drafted. In this case, however, the Supreme Administrative Court judges expressed their disapproval of the manner in which the amendment to the act was created. The judges of the Supreme Administrative Court addressed a so-called alert to the Prime Minister of the Government, pointing out the failure to observe the principles of lawmaking in amending the act. However, this alert does not seem to have positively influenced lawmaking in Poland.

However, determining the amount of the tax still gave rise to doubts. In the case of entities depreciating their assets, the tax base for structures is the initial value calculated for tax depreciation purposes. This does not apply when a structure is not depreciated—in which case, the taxable base is determined by its market value. No item in the fixed asset register corresponds to the entire wind power plant. Individual elements of the power plant were depreciated; as a result, the market value had to be the wind power plant's tax base. The dispute concerned the following questions:

- At what point in time should this value be determined?
- Should this point be the moment when the wind power plant was built (at which time a tax liability arose in relation to its construction part), or only at the beginning of 2017, when the entire wind power plant was taxed?

[7] I SA/Bd 866/16.

[8] I SA/Go 56/17.

[9] I SA/Ol 17/17.

[10] I SA/Rz 233/17.

[11] Judgement of the Provincial Administrative Court in Gorzów Wielkopolski of 8 March 2017, I SA/Go 56/17.

[12] II FSK 2983/17.

Taxpayers argued that the taxable base for wind turbines in 2017 should be their market value determined as of 1 January 2017 because this date is when the legislature created a completely new taxable structure. The administrative courts have accepted this approach.[13]

These changes resulted in the tax burden on wind farms increasing by about four times. This activity could not generate profits that would encourage further investment. It even threatened to close existing wind power plants. Taxpayers could sell unprofitable wind power plants at low prices. The entity that would buy such a power plant would pay a tax on the purchase price since this purchase price would be the plant's market price. As a result, municipalities would not benefit at all from the increase in the tax burden on wind power plants. This change constituted a surprising example of a legal regulation that did not benefit anyone.

6.5 Yet the Government Likes Wind Turbines?

When the seven judges of the Supreme Administrative Court issued their judgement, the legal situation had already changed. By virtue of the Act on Amendments to the Act on Renewable Energy Sources and Certain Other Acts of 7 June 2018,[14] another change in the legal regulation was made. This time, the changes were again reversed, but the changes introduced by the Act of 20 June 2016 were also reversed. After these changes, a wind power plant was deemed to comprise two elements: a structure, which consists only of construction parts, and 'technical equipment, [...] in which electricity is generated from wind energy'. Additionally, the phrase 'wind turbines' was reinstated in Article 3(3) of the C.L.A. This update meant that, again, only the construction part of a wind turbine should be taxed.

However, these changes were only relevant to existing wind power plants or wind power plants that were currently under construction. High tax burdens have ceased to threaten their existence. However, restrictions under—inter alia—the 10H rule still apply. The government has stopped fighting wind power plants, but this newfound tolerance does not mean that it has taken a liking to them.

6.6 The Retroactivity of the Change in Taxation Rules for Wind Power Plants

However, even reasonable changes to legal regulations can also give rise to serious doubts. This time, a problem concerned the issue of the regulation changes' temporal scope. The amendment to the W.P.P.A. entered into force as of 1 January 2018—that is, retroactively. From taxpayers' point of view, this solution was partially beneficial

[13] Judgement of the Supreme Administrative Court of 4 February 2020, II FSK 2584/19.

[14] Journal of Laws of 2018, item 1276.

even though they were still burdened with an unreasonably high real estate tax in relation to 2017.

Municipalities' position, however, differed considerably. Municipal tax authorities had already collected real estate tax payments for almost half of 2018; often, this money had already been spent. Returning these funds presented a financial problem, especially since wind energy investments are often located in poorly urbanised, usually poor areas. In such municipalities, tax revenues from wind turbines could constitute a significant budget item. Moreover, a serious legal problem arose. Simply put, Polish tax regulations do not at all regulate the procedure of refunding tax payments that were collected legally and then became undue.

This matter also has a constitutional aspect. In Poland, undoubtedly, a retroactive amendment to tax law is, in principle, inadmissible. It may occur exceptionally, but only in the taxpayer's favour (Wierczyński, 2016).

From this perspective, a retroactive change to the scope of taxing wind power plants in the taxpayer's favour was permissible even if, under civil law, the municipality is a legal entity separate from the state. From a citizen's point of view, both the state and a municipality are public entities, constituting different forms of state authority (Morawski & Kałążny, 2021, p. 10). In the judgement of 22 July 2020,[15] the Constitutional Tribunal found that such a regulation violates the constitutional principle of the prohibition of the retroactivity of law, which the tribunal based on Article 2 of the Constitution of the Republic of Poland and the principle of a democratic legal state contained therein. This finding does not mean that municipalities were given the right to refuse to refund tax payments for 2018 or to demand refunds from taxpayers of tax payments that the municipality had already refunded under the 2018 amendment to the W.P.P.A. The reasoning of the Constitutional Tribunal's judgement clarifies that it expects to compensate municipalities for the amendment's effects. The judgement has, therefore, not resolved much.

The Act of 17 November 2021 is likely to end the disputes concerning the compensation of revenues lost by municipalities in 2018 due to the change in the taxation scope for wind power plants.[16] The law grants municipalities the right to full compensation for the effects of the reduction of the tax burden on wind power plants' retroactive introduction. Making sense of the related disputes as a whole is difficult.

[15] K 4/19.

[16] Journal of Laws of 2022, item 30.

Chapter 7
The Taxation of Land Used for Energy Production

Abstract The provisions of the L.T.C.A. governing land taxation introduce a general rule that land on which actual business activities are undertaken is taxed more heavily than other land. Apart from a purely fiscal function (a higher tax for entrepreneurs who derive profits from the land), this solution also plays a stimulation role in that the tax regulation encourages the taxpayer to occupy the land for business activity only in such an area and for such a time as are necessary. This condition is particularly important in the case of opencast mining, which has a particularly heavy impact on the landscape. The regulations in force motivate entrepreneurs to restore the land as quickly as possible as part of the reclamation process. In this context, whether protective strips are treated as occupied for business activity may be subject to doubts. Imposing maximum tax rates on such land discourages taxpayers from voluntarily surrounding their power plants or mines with a 'green buffer'. On the contrary, entrepreneurs can profit by using the maximum legal area of their land if they pay the same tax on this land as they would on unused land. Therefore, this interpretation of the legislation not only fails to fulfil its protective function with respect to the land but may even have the opposite effect.

Keywords Land · Land occupied for business activity · Land connected with business activity · Land reclamation · Open cast mines · Photovoltaic farm

7.1 Introduction

Land taxation plays an important role in sectors where business activity requires the occupation of large areas of land. This role undoubtedly applies to opencast mineral extraction; therefore, a significant number of disputes concerning the interpretation of the key issue of land taxation—that is, 'occupation for business activity'—can be observed in this industry, especially in the context of the reclamation process. The issue of land taxation also affects the taxation of energy production activities, and it is proportionally more important for renewable energy (particularly photovoltaics) than for conventional power plants.

W. Morawski and A. Kałążny, *The Taxation of Energy-Sector Assets: Polish Tax Legislation on the Eve of Energy Transformation*, SpringerBriefs in Energy,
https://doi.org/10.1007/978-3-031-15673-1_7

7.2 Land Occupied for the Extraction of Energy Resources

Land owned by an entrepreneur is most often taxed with the real estate tax rate for land connected with business activity, regardless of how it is classified in the register of land and buildings (Article 5(1)(1)(a) of the L.T.C.A.). For 2022, this rate has been set to PLN 1.03 per 1 m^2 of area (although individual municipalities may introduce lower rates according to Article 5(1) of the L.T.C.A.).

At the same time, the L.T.C.A. provides for specific situations in which land may not be subject to taxation, taking advantage of exclusion or exemption. In particular, pursuant to Article 2(2) of the L.T.C.A., agricultural land or forests—with the exception of those occupied for business activities—are not subject to the real estate tax. Pursuant to Article 7(1)(10) of the L.T.C.A., wasteland, ecological land, wooded land and bushes—with the exception of land occupied for business activities—is exempt from the real estate tax. In both cases, in order to take advantage of the taxation exclusion or exemption, two conditions must be jointly fulfilled: first, the appropriate classification in the land register (as agricultural land, forests, wasteland, ecological land, wooded land or bushes) and, second, the lack of occupation for business activity. The second condition raises more doubts since the notion of 'occupation for business activity' lacks a legal definition. Therefore, the meaning of this term, which is crucial from the land taxation perspective, should be determined on the basis of a linguistic interpretation grounded in colloquial language.

Both the Polish tax law doctrine and the jurisprudence accept that the recognition of land as occupied for business activity requires that specific activities be performed on it, which is consistent with the dictionary definition of the word 'occupy': to fill with oneself or with something, some space, area (Dubisz, 2003). Nevertheless, such an understanding of the word 'occupation' may raise doubts in practice, given the diversity of objects and forms of business activity performed by various entrepreneurs. This problem was pointed out by the Supreme Administrative Court. For example, in the judgement of 26 September 2018,[1] concerning the taxation of land belonging to a holiday resort, the court indicated that the scope of the notion of 'occupation for the purpose of carrying out economic activity' should be understood in an individualised manner, taking into account the specificity of a given type of activity. This individual specificity plays a significant role in the tax settlements of opencast mines. To conduct their activity, they occupy very large areas of land, which are often classified in the land register as *agricultural land* or *forests*; therefore, the issue of taxation of grounds is particularly important for such mines. Undoubtedly, the land on which mining is conducted is considered to be occupied. The jurisprudence has also established an approach according to which land occupation for mining ends with the issuance of a decision on the completion of reclamation (as, inter alia, in the Supreme Administrative Court judgement of 4 *April* 2019[2]). (For more on the issue of reclamation in this chapter, see Sect. 7.4: 'Land Reclamation'). Problematically, however, the point at which land occupation starts remains ambiguous.

---

[1] II FSK 2771/16.

[2] II FSK 1021/17.

According to some courts, land is occupied for business activity from the moment a mining concession is issued that lists the land as part of a mining area (e.g. in the judgement of the Provincial Administrative Court in Gliwice of 20 January 2015[3]). This position contradicts the jurisprudence to date, which—as mentioned above in this section—has indicated that, before land occupation can be established, actual actions must be undertaken on the land. Meanwhile, assuming that the mere fact of including land in concession documents is sufficient to establish land occupation for business activity would mean breaking with the previously established approach and recognition that legal and not merely factual circumstances sufficiently indicate occupation.

In this context, the judgement of the Supreme Administrative Court of 2 September 2020 plays an important role.[4] The judgement recalled the correct way to interpret the term 'occupied for business activity'. As the court pointed out, 'occupied' is understood only as land on which actual business activity has been carried out via physical occupation. In the Supreme Administrative Court's opinion, organisational or legal actions are not manifestations of business occupation. Importantly, as an example of a formal and legal activity which does not prejudge the occupation of land (in the absence of actual actions), the court pointed to the obtainment of a building permit.

The judgement of 2 September 2020 referred to above is also practically significant, and not only for opencast mines, since it concerns land that belongs to a deep coal mine. The concession documents that define the mining area in question indicate the numbers of the land plots under which the pit is located. For this reason, the tax authorities assumed that all the plots listed in the concession documents should be considered to be occupied for business activities since, according to the concession documents, they are located in a mining area. Pursuant to Article 6(1)(5) of G.M.L.A., a 'mining area' is understood as a space within the boundaries of which an entrepreneur is authorised, in particular, to mine a mineral and carry out the mining works necessary to fulfil the licence. However, the Supreme Administrative Court agreed with taxpayers' position that land located on the surface above a deep mine should not be considered to be occupied for business purposes because deep mining does not (as a rule) interfere with the ground surface. On the other hand, the mining area is not a surface but a three-dimensional, solid space that extends deep into the Earth and that ends where the land begins. And yet, the boundaries of the land property extend as far as the contact between the land and the mineral deposit, which is already subject to separate ownership and does not constitute a component of the land property (Schwartz, 2012).

Accordingly, in the case of deep mines, the problem of land taxation can be assumed not to arise in principle, except for the area occupied by the mine's surface infrastructure (mine shafts, a processing plant etc.). The area of land occupied by a spoil and waste (waste rock) dump site should also be considered as occupied for a deep mine's business activity. For an area occupied by a waste rock dump site, the

[3] I SA/Gl 201/14.

[4] II FSK 1520/18.

same tax rules generally apply as for opencast mine workings. The area would be considered to be occupied for business purposes from the moment waste is deposited on it until the moment reclamation is completed.

In the case of land used to extract other energy resources (oil and gas), the issue of land taxation generally plays a minor role because of the relatively small land area occupied by this type of activity (compared to opencast lignite mines).

7.3 Land Occupied for Energy Production

The issue of taxing land occupied by conventional power plants can be, in principle, compared to the situation of any other production plant. A specific issue that arises in relation to the land associated with energy production is the taxation of the protective strips around power plants (although, notably, this issue also applies to other industries, particularly large industrial plants).

Due to power plants' impact on their surroundings, protection strips of various widths are set up around these facilities. Due to current technologies, and particularly the reduction in dust emissions, conventional power plants' impact on their surroundings is much less significant than in the past, which also limits protection strips' role. Nevertheless, these strips' taxation issue may be materially significant if Poland's planned nuclear power plant is built.[5]

Protective strips often include land classified as a forest or agricultural land; therefore, in order for these strips to be properly classified for tax purposes, whether they should be regarded as occupied for the purpose of conducting business activity should be determined (which, in turn, determines whether they are subject to or excluded from the real estate tax and subject to the much lower forest or agricultural tax). The jurisprudence generally accepts that a protective strip should be considered as an area occupied for business activity. For example, the Supreme Administrative Court judgement of 30 May 2017[6] indicated that the agricultural land located in a protective strip is occupied for business activity. The court considered, in particular, the taxpayer's undertaking of activities on the land (fencing and tree cutting), as well as the lack of agricultural activity on the land, as arguments for this qualification. The doctrine presents a view according to which the land in the protective strip should not be qualified as occupied for business activity if it is used for agricultural activity, which excludes conducting business activity on the same land (Dowgier et al., 2021).[7] The doctrine also indicates that the land within a protective strip is occupied for the purpose of conducting business activity but that this condition is not tantamount to recognising that the land is occupied for this activity (Morawski,

[5] https://www.gov.pl/web/polski-atom/program-polskiej-energetyki-jadrowej, retrieved 23 May 2022.

[6] II FSK 1014/15.

[7] https://sip.lex.pl/#/commentary/587865025/662465/dowgier-rafal-i-in-podatki-i-oplaty-lokalne-komentarz?keyword=pas%20ochronny%20podatek&cm=SREST, retrieved 26 May 2022.

2009, p. 297). This indication leads to the conclusion that such land may, at most, be regarded as connected to conducting business activity (but not occupied), which does not exclude its taxation via the agricultural or forestry tax.

In this context, we must point to the provisions of the Act of 20 May 2016 on investments in wind power plants.[8] Inter alia, these provisions regulate the rules for new power plants' location. Pursuant to Article 4(1) of this Act, a wind power plant may be built in relation to a residential building only at a distance equal to or greater than ten times the plant's height. This provision delineates such a wide area of 'wind power free zones' that the development of wind energy in Poland has halted due to the few sites that could meet the requirement for an adequate distance from residential buildings.[9] The question arises of whether the logic presented in the jurisprudence we have cited on protective strips should not be transferred to the case of specific 'protection zones' delimited around wind power plants. Of course, this application would lead to absurd results—that is, the (alleged) occupation of huge areas of the country for business activity.

Land taxation is an important issue for photovoltaic farms, which occupy large areas (tens or even hundreds of hectares) that are often classified as agricultural land or wasteland and, therefore, subject to the real estate tax only for the portion considered to be occupied for business activities. When determining 'business occupation', a photovoltaic farm's area can be divided into different zones in terms of the intensity and permanence of the activities actually undertaken on the land.

In principle, one area that is unquestionably occupied for business purposes is—of course—the area underneath the pylons that constitute the support elements for photovoltaic panels, but this area will account for a very small proportion of an entire photovoltaic farm. More doubts arise in the case of an area on which such a farm's supporting elements are not built that is, at the same time, shielded by panels above. Because panels are sometimes installed a few metres above ground level, the area beneath them may be used for activities other than energy production—particularly various activities related to agriculture, such as goat and sheep grazing or beekeeping. Taxpayers have presented the conducting of such activities under panels as an argument that this area is not occupied to conduct business activity; however, administrative courts have challenged this suggestion so far.[10] The jurisprudence's position in this respect raises doubts as to its compliance with the regulations because, as we have already indicated in this section's discussion concerning protective strips, the doctrine accepts that conducting non-economic activity on the land (e.g. farming) precludes the land's classification as *occupied*.

The final type of land used by a photovoltaic farm is the uncovered area between rows of panels and the space between such a farm's installations and its plot's boundaries. On such land, no actual business activity is undertaken, nor can the ability to use this land—for example, for agricultural activity—be restricted in any way. However,

---

[8] Journal of Laws 2016, item 961.

[9] https://mojafirma.infor.pl/ekobiznes/5269291,Ustawa-odleglosciowa-Czy-wiatraki-beda-budowane-blizej.html, retrieved 26 May 2022.

[10] Judgement of the Provincial Administrative Court in Warsaw of 7 May 2019, III SA/Wa 1932/18.

the prevailing view of the jurisprudence suggests that a photovoltaic farm's land should be regarded as occupied for business purposes, even the portion where panels (or any other technical infrastructure) are not located, because this area is necessarily used to achieve the operation's intended result—that is, the installation and operation of a photovoltaic farm in order to generate electricity.[11] Rather, the arguments raised by the courts seem to support the consideration of this land as associated with the activity of electricity production but not as occupation for the sake of this activity (Kałążny & Jankowska, 2022, pp. 39–45).

7.4 Land Reclamation

Any economic activity may lead to some land degradation. Once an activity has finished, such damage must usually be remediated unless the land continues to be used for economic activities. This problem is particularly acute in the case of certain energy-related activities which considerably disturb the land. An extreme example is lignite mining, which involves the construction of huge opencast mines. The decommissioning of such a mine is a long and costly undertaking that sometimes does not lead to the land's full restoration to its original state.[12] This process usually occurs gradually while a mine is still operating—then, of course, final reclamation efforts occur on land where lignite mining has already ceased. Land reclamation is an obligation owing to the provisions of the Act of 3 February 1995 on the protection of agricultural and forest land.[13]

For many years, administrative courts' verdicts have effectively established a line of jurisprudence which is unfavourable for taxpayers concerning the issue of taxing land associated with the event of reclamation. The judgement of the Supreme Administrative Court of 9 December 2016 may constitute an example.[14] The court's view can be summarised as follows: since reclamation is a necessary consequence of business activity, reclaimed land is not only associated with business activity but even occupied for the sake of conducting business activity; therefore, such land is taxed at a relatively high real estate tax rate—higher than the rate that applies to land that is not associated with business activity. This thesis was repeated in a significant number of judgements by administrative courts.[15]

This position has been treated as established in jurisprudence, but it does not follow directly from the law. No provision had said that land which is not used to generate earnings (which is, after all, the essence of business activity) is still associated with

[11] Judgement of the Provincial Administrative Court in Kielce of 9 September 2021, I SA/Ke 235/21; Judgement of the Provincial Administrative Court in Rzeszów of 8 June 2021, I SA/Rz 287/21.

[12] Due to the depth of an opencast mine, backfilling such mines is often impossible, so reclamation sometimes leads to the creation of an artificial body of water.

[13] Journal of Laws of 2021, item 1326 as amended.

[14] II FSK 3332/14.

[15] Judgement of the Provincial Administrative Court in Poznan of 25 October 2017, I SA/Po 628/17.

business activity. This line of jurisprudence should now, seemingly, be considered outdated. However, the above considerations regarding connection with business activity concern the past. Significant changes were effected by the verdict of the Constitutional Tribunal of 24 February 2021,[16] according to which:

> Article 1a(1)(3) of the Act of 12 January 1991 on local taxes and charges (*Journal of Laws of 2019*, item 1170), understood in such a way that the connection of land, building or structure with the conduct of business activity is determined exclusively by the possession of land, building or structure by an entrepreneur or other entity conducting business activity, is inconsistent with Article 64(1) in connection with Article 31(3) and Article 84 of the Constitution of the Republic of Poland.

The verdict of the Constitutional Tribunal of 24 February 2021 removed a significant part of the legal definition of 'land, buildings and structures connected with the conduct of business activity'. The basic positive criterion for qualifying the subject of taxation to this category—that is, possession by the entrepreneur—disappeared. Thus, indeed, this notion currently lack a definition, and only the exceptions specified in Article 1a(2a) of the L.T.C.A. remain. Therefore, this concept must be reconstructed based on the individual meanings of the words it comprises.

Reclamation is seldom doubted as an activity that should be taken into account when conducting business activities using land. Article 20(1) of the Law on Protection of Agricultural Land reads, 'The person who causes the loss or reduction of the use-value of the land shall be obliged to recultivate it at his own expense'. And according to Article 20(3) of this law, 'Land reclamation and development shall be planned, designed and implemented at all stages of industrial activity'. Thus, reclamation can hypothetically take place during business activities on land that is even still in use.

However, the key provision of the Law on Protection of Agricultural Land is Article 20(4), according to which, 'Land reclamation shall be carried out as and when the land becomes totally, partially or temporarily redundant for industrial activities and shall be completed within 5 years after the cessation of such activities'.

This provision acquires significance in the context of the Constitutional Tribunal judgement of 24 February 2021. Once land becomes redundant for business activity, the only factor connecting it to business activity is the individual holder or owner, who is an entrepreneur. The land was previously used to generate income, but is no longer a source of income.

Remember that the criterion for increasing the tax burden in the real estate tax is 'some' connection with business activity—which, however, in the light of the judgement of the Constitutional Tribunal, must be considered in the context of the principle of proportionality. Increasing the tax burden on the basis of the formal criterion of the entrepreneur's possession was disproportionate. The tribunal expects a stronger link to economic activity which is not only formal but also real. However, in the case under consideration, the land was no longer useful for this activity since it was subject to reclamation. It no longer generated any income and, for the entrepreneur, was just encumbrance.

[16] SK 39/19.

Any connection 'with the conduct of business activity' is difficult to observe when this activity has ceased (Article 20(4) of the Law on the Protection of Agricultural Land). Of course, the entrepreneur had not ceased activity in general, but he had ceased 'this activity'—that is, the activity carried out on this land. This situation is analogous to a situation already analysed by the Constitutional Tribunal. In both cases, the entity was an entrepreneur who conducts activity 'somewhere else', not on this particular land which was a subject to tax dispute. And, in both cases, the land should be deemed to be no longer 'connected with conducting business activity'. At most, it is associated with former business activity.

This conclusion abundantly clarifies that, following the Constitutional Tribunal judgement of 24 February 2021, the administrative courts must rethink their earlier rulings (leaving aside even the question of whether they were justified in the legal context at the time). Of course, from the environmental protection perspective, this solution may be controversial because it does not encourage the entrepreneur to reclaim the land quickly.

The problem of long-lasting recultivation processes sometimes lies in the administration's practice. The administration assigns the key role in the decision on the determination of reclamation efforts' completion. Recultivation is assumed to end only on this date. Unfortunately, in practice, municipalities try to extend the process of issuing this decision (it is not issued by municipal authorities) based on trivial reasons. As a result, sometimes several years after the actual end of recultivation, land is treated as if it were still being recultivated.

Chapter 8
Offshore Wind Farms: A Special Tax Regime

Abstract The considerations presented in this chapter have shown the difficulty of finding a solution that would, on the one hand, remove the loophole preventing the taxation of offshore wind farms and, on the other hand, remain compliant with the constitutional standards of tax lawmaking. The adopted solution allows legislators to achieve their objective of similar tax treatment for all electricity production methods. This goal has been achieved first by fixing concession fees to an amount which corresponds with the load of an onshore wind farm. The resultant constitutional problems were primarily caused by the de facto concealment of the tax under the name of a 'concession fee'. Meanwhile, based on the Polish Constitution, the name of the service is not important but, rather, its features. Since this fee bears the features of a tax, it should first be regulated by a statute, whereas the adopted solution enables the fee amount to be determined by way of regulation. A moderate risk of recognising the regulation as violating the constitution has resulted from this approach. Another effect of replacing the real estate tax with a concession fee is to change the beneficiary of the income in question. While the real estate tax contributes to a municipal budget, the concession fee contributes to the central budget. Therefore, for taxpayers, the introduction of this fee is an economically neutral solution. (The amount has been established to correspond to the amount of the real estate tax paid for onshore wind farms.) But municipalities that counted on revenues from taxing offshore wind farms are disadvantaged by the adopted solution.

Keywords Offshore · Offshore windfarm · Concession fee · Exclusive economic zone

8.1 Offshore Wind Farms: The Problem of Building in 'No Man's Land'

Renewable energy is an important source of the tax revenues collected by local authorities in Poland. We have described how heated disputes between tax authorities and taxpayers may arise in the case of wind power plants in Chap. 6: 'The Taxation of Wind Power Plants: A Case of Regulatory Instability'. From this perspective,

W. Morawski and A. Kałążny, *The Taxation of Energy-Sector Assets: Polish Tax Legislation on the Eve of Energy Transformation*, SpringerBriefs in Energy,
https://doi.org/10.1007/978-3-031-15673-1_8

that offshore wind farms became an interest in the doctrine of Polish tax law many years before the first actual investments in this industry appeared is unsurprising (Pahl, 2003, pp. 40–44). Due to offshore wind farms' very high investment value, municipalities—which are both tax authorities and the beneficiaries of the real estate tax—were vitally interested in taxing potential offshore wind farms. For this type of investment, the construction part that constitutes the tax base of the wind farm structure (which is undoubtedly subject to the real estate tax) could reach a very high value due to significant costs related to the construction of windmills at sea. The main discussion, however, concerned not the tax base for offshore wind farms (as was the case for onshore farms) but determining to whom and according to what rates, if any, the tax would be paid.

In accordance with Article 2(1) of the Act on Maritime Areas, the maritime areas of the Republic of Poland comprise: (1) internal marine waters, (2) the territorial sea, (3) the contiguous zone and (4) the Exclusive Economic Zone.[1] The territory of Poland is composed of internal sea waters and the territorial sea.[2] A contrario, therefore, the Exclusive Economic Zone (where offshore wind farms are located) is not the territory of Poland but artificial islands, structures and equipment which are used, inter alia, for energy purposes are subject to Polish law.[3] Since structures erected in the Exclusive Economic Zone are subject to Polish law, they should be considered a potential subject of the real estate tax, and offshore wind farms include structures which meet the definition of a 'taxable structure'.

The regulations in force enable the determination of which tax authority is suitable for levying the real estate tax on objects in the Polish Exclusive Economic Zone. As a rule, the tax authority qualified to rule on the real estate tax is the head of the municipality (*gmina*) in which the taxable objects are located.[4] Admittedly, no municipal authority is responsible for the Exclusive Economic Zone (which does not constitute the territory of Poland and so does not fall within the area of any municipality either) however, according to the relevant executive regulations of the Polish Tax Ordinance, if the local responsibility cannot be determined in the manner indicated in the provisions of the tax law, the tax authority responsible for local taxation matters is the President of the Capital City of Warsaw.[5] However, the determination of the competent tax authority would not enable the tax to be levied when the tax rate is still unspecified.

The reason for the problem regarding finding of the proper tax rate was that the real estate tax is a local tax. The law provides only for maximum tax rates, and the rates applicable in a given municipality are set by the municipality itself through a resolution of its municipal council.[6] A resolution of a municipal council, as an act of

[1] Journal of Laws of 2022, item 457, 1079.

[2] Article 2(2), Maritime Areas Act.

[3] Article 22, paragraph 2, Maritime Areas Act.

[4] Article 1c, Article 6(7) and Article 6(9) of the L.T.C.A.

[5] Section 10 of the Ordinance of the Minister of Finance of 22 August 2005 on the jurisdiction of tax authorities, Journal of Laws 2019, item 2371.

[6] Article 5(1), L.T.C.A.

local law, is a source of universally binding law only within the territory of the given municipality.[7] Therefore, to determine the tax rate applicable to an offshore wind farm structure, one should identify the resolution issued by the municipal council whose area includes the Polish Exclusive Economic Zone. However, the Exclusive Economic Zone, as an area which does not constitute the territory of the Republic of Poland, is not the territory of any municipality in Poland; consequently, it is not the purview of any municipal council. The rates resulting from the L.T.C.A. cannot be applied in this context since this regulation addresses municipalities and only limits their freedom to shape tax burdens.

The lack of taxation for offshore wind farms, alongside the simultaneous taxation of their onshore counterparts, causes potential problems even beyond the lack of tax revenue for municipalities. Entrepreneurs' different legal situations in analogous situations may sometimes be treated as state aid.[8] Of course, even if offshore wind power plants were completely untaxed, such an 'exemption' would be very unlikely to be considered state aid. But the very risk of such a consideration must worry investors. Note that EU member states can also pursue their tax policies using a tax's stimulative function. From this perspective, taxing renewable energy more favourably than carbon-intensive energy would be, in principle, acceptable from the perspective of state aid rules. However, even at the grounds of national law, one might doubt whether the lack of taxation for offshore wind power plants infringes upon the constitutional principle of equality.[9]

8.2 Concession Fees

The legal loophole preventing the taxation of offshore wind farms for many years was a problem with no negative consequences for either public finances or respecting the principle of entrepreneurs' equality, given the absence of offshore wind farms in the Polish Exclusive Economic Zone. However, concrete investment plans announced by energy corporations in 2019 motivated Polish legislators to address this problem. Indeed, investments in offshore wind farms located in the Polish Exclusive Economic Zone have attracted strong interest from the largest Polish and global energy companies, including joint projects by Poland's Polenergia and Norway's Equinor, joint projects by Poland's Grupa Energetyczna and Denmark's Orsred and a joint project by Poland's Orlen and Canada's Northland Power, as well as projects by Germany's RWE and the French-Spanish project by EDPR and Engie.[10]

---

[7] Article 87(2) of the Polish Constitution.

[8] Articles 107–109 of the Treaty on the Functioning of the European Union.

[9] Article 32 of the Polish Constitution.

[10] https://biznesalert.pl/morskie-farmy-wiatrowe-wnioski-o-wsparcie-offshore-ure-oze-energetyka/; https://www.ure.gov.pl/pl/urzad/informacje-ogolne/aktualnosci/9388,Offshore-Prezes-Urzedu-Regulacji-Energetyki-rozpatrzyl-pierwsze-wnioski-w-ramach.html; https://www.ure.gov.pl/pl/urzad/informacje-ogolne/aktualnosci/9436,Offshore-Prezes-Urzedu-Regulacji-Energetyki-rozpatrzyl-kolejne-dwa-wnioski-w-ram.html, retrieved 26 May 2022.

Legislators intended to close this loophole and eliminate its negative consequences. First, it resulted in the inequality of onshore wind farms (as well as other onshore energy sources), for which the real estate tax is a significant cost of business.[11] Secondly, it deprived the budget of important tax revenues.

The chosen solution was presented in the government's draft of the law on the promotion of electricity generation in offshore wind farms, which was finally submitted to Parliament and adopted as the Law of 17 December 2020 on the promotion of electricity generation in offshore wind farms.[12] This solution chosen by Polish legislators consists, in its introduction, of a concession fee paid by an energy company performing an economic activity in the field of electricity generation at an offshore wind farm (hereinafter: the 'concession fee for an offshore wind farm'). The new concession fee is regulated by the modified provisions of the Energy Law Act of 10 March 1997.[13]

The subject of the concession fee for an offshore wind farm is the performance of business activity in the field of electricity generation at an offshore wind farm referred to in the Act of 17 December 2020 on the promotion of electricity generation at offshore wind farms (this act contains a definition of an 'offshore wind farm'[14]).

The concession fee itself, related to energy production, is not novel in Polish law. An entrepreneur wishing to engage in the activity of generating electricity pays such a concession fee, which is a product of the energy company's revenue obtained through the sale of goods or services within the scope of its activity covered by the concession and achieved during the year in which the obligation to pay the fee arose, as well as an appropriate coefficient, defined in the regulations issued pursuant to Article 34(6) of E.L.A. (hereinafter: the 'concession fee for energy generation'). Currently in force is the Ordinance of the Council of Ministers of 9 November 2018 on this concession fee,[15] according to which—in the case of electricity generation—this coefficient is 0.0005. Essentially, therefore, the concession fee is a kind of revenue tax at a rate of 0.05%.

An energy enterprise performing an economic activity of producing electric energy at an offshore wind farm pays a concession fee constituting the sum of the above-mentioned concession fee for energy generation and an amount constituting a specific 'supplement' to this fee (this supplement is referred to hereinafter as the 'concession fee for an offshore wind farm'). It is calculated as a product of the installed electric capacity of the offshore wind farm, expressed in megawatts (MW), resulting from the licence for the production of electrical energy at this offshore wind farm, and an appropriate coefficient, expressed in PLN, specified in the regulations

---

[11] Rządowe Centrum Legislacji. (23 December 2019). Explanatory memorandum to the draft law on promoting electricity generation in offshore wind farms. https://legislacja.gov.pl/projekt/12329105/katalog/12656009#12656009, retrieved 15 April 2021.

[12] *Journal of Laws 2021*, Item 234, cited hereinafter as 'the Offshore Wind Farms Act'.

[13] Article 34 of the Act of 10 April 1997—Energy Law, Journal of Laws of 2021, item 716, hereinafter cited as the 'Energy Law' or 'E.L.A.'.

[14] Article 3(3) of O.W.F.A.t.

[15] Journal of Laws 2018, item 2277.

issued pursuant to Article 34, Paragraph 6, of E.L.A.[16] The act stipulates that this coefficient cannot exceed PLN 23,000.[17] The executive regulation determining the amount of the coefficient set it at PLN 23,000—that is, the maximum permissible amount.[18]

The amount of the coefficient (23,000 PLN) was determined on the basis of a comparative analysis of the real estate tax costs incurred by onshore wind farms, as indicated in the justification of the draft law on offshore wind farms prepared by the Council of Ministers[19]:

> The amount of the coefficient in question is estimated at 23,000 PLN/MW, taking into account the balancing of the fiscal burden of offshore and onshore wind technologies, as the difference between:
>
> (a) the average level of real estate tax for onshore wind farms, amounting to PLN 36,000/MW per year, less
> (b) the average fee for the issuance of permits to erect and exploit artificial islands, installations and equipment in Polish maritime areas for offshore wind farms under the Act on Maritime Areas of the Republic of Poland and Maritime Administration, calculated per one year of operation of the project, amounting to PLN 5000/MW/year, and
> (c) the average real estate tax resulting from the application of 2% real estate tax to the assessed value of the onshore part of the offshore wind farm infrastructure, amounting to PLN 8000/MW/year.

Pursuant to Article 34(7) of E.L.A., an energy company producing electricity through a renewable energy source installation with the total capacity of the renewable energy source installation not exceeding 5 MW is exempted from paying a concession fee on the production of energy in that installation.

8.3 The Sea Occupation Concession Fee

The concession fee described above, related to the construction and operation of the wind farm, is linked to the permit fee for the occupation of the Exclusive Economic Zone for the erection and use of artificial islands, structures and equipment, mentioned in the Law on Maritime Areas.[20]

[16] Article 34(2)(2a) of E.L.A..

[17] Article 34(2a) of E.L.A.. The amount of PLN 23,000 is equivalent to EUR 4,922, according to the exchange rate of 20 June 2022.

[18] Regulation of the Council of Ministers of 12 October 2021 on the concession fee (*Journal of Laws 2021*, item 1938).

[19] https://www.sejm.gov.pl/Sejm9.nsf/PrzebiegProc.xsp?id=0282D90367CB9DADC12586370030F731, retrieved 26 May 2022.

[20] It is further described as a 'concession fee for the occupation of maritime areas', though such a term is not used in the Maritime Areas Act, which uses a simpler term: 'concession fee'.

In principle, the concession fee for the permit to work within the maritime area is only PLN 1500. If the issued permit concerns the occupation of the Exclusive Economic Zone for the erection and use of artificial islands, constructions and devices, the entity which was granted the permit would pay an additional fee amounting to 1% of the value of the planned undertaking (this fee is referred to as 'the concession fee for the occupation of the Exclusive Economic Zone').[21] The value of the planned project is calculated for the purpose of the additional fee, taking into account market prices for the equipment and services necessary to completely execute the project as of the date of submitting the application for the permit.[22] The additional fee is paid gradually, as follows:

1. 10% of the full amount of the fee within 90 days of the date on which the permit decision becomes final,
2. 30% of the full amount within 30 days from that date,
3. 30% of the full amount within 30 days of the date on which the use of artificial islands, structures and equipment began, and
4. 30% of the full amount after three years from the date of the payment referred to in Point 3.

Therefore, this fee is not strictly a permit fee since it need not always be paid (e.g. in the event of abandonment) even if a permit is granted.

8.4 The Concession Fee as a Tax Substitute

The concession fees described above in Sect. 8.2. were introduced as substitutes for the real estate tax, which would be payable for a wind farm if (hypothetically) the Exclusive Economic Zone were treated as a typical part of Polish territory. This solution resulted in a similar tax burden on offshore and onshore wind farms. However, it may not be clear why did legislators not decide to tax offshore wind farms, introducing instead a model of taxing them with concession fees.

We should point out that legislators originally planned to introduce a new tax (rather than a concession fee) on offshore wind farms. It would not be a local tax and, therefore, would not require a municipal council to adopt its rates. This idea was presented in a draft law prepared by the Minister of State Assets on the promotion of electricity generation in offshore wind farms dated 23 December 2019.[23] The draft provided for the introduction of a 'tax on offshore wind farms', the object of which would be the conduct of business activity in the field of electricity generation at an offshore wind farm. The tax base would have resulted from the concession of the installed electrical capacity of the offshore wind farm, while the tax rate was

---

[21] Article 27b(1) of the Law on Maritime Areas.

[22] Article 27b(1d), Law on Maritime Areas.

[23] https://legislacja.gov.pl/docs//2/12329105/12656009/12656010/dokument434588.pdf, retrieved 12 April 2021.

to be set as a lump sum of PLN 23,000 per 1 MW. The tax was to constitute state budget revenue, while the responsible tax authorities were to be the tax administration authorities relevant according to the taxpayer's place of residence (not the location of the offshore wind farm).

A number of comments were submitted to the presented draft as part of public consultations.[24] Among them, the most frequent concern was the mechanism for the annual adjustment of the flat-rate tax amount included in the provisions. Commenters pointed out that the provisions on the real estate tax do not provide for the valorisation of the tax rate on structures.[25] Generally, the tax base—which is the initial value of the structure for tax depreciation purposes—also remained unchanged. According to the intention of the legislation's authors, the amount of tax levied on offshore wind farms should correspond to the amount of real estate tax paid on land-based power plants. Consequently, the introduction of the valorisation mechanism was, indeed, illogical. Another issue that was noted after the draft was analysed was entrusting the responsibility to issue a de facto decision determining the amount of the tax base to a non-tax-related authority (the President of the Energy Regulatory Office issuing an energy production concession), which a taxpayer could not challenge with the responsible tax authority (which is bound by the concession's content) (Ruta, 2020, p. 58).

The adopted legislative solution raises some constitutional problems. In analysing the nature of the concession feefor offshore wind farm, one may conclude that it does actually constitute a tax. In Poland, fees are payable for some kind of mutual benefit to the state or a local government administration; therefore, they are equivalent (Gomułowicz, 2008, p. 137). Neither the concession fee for offshore wind farms nor the concession fee for the occupation of maritime areas existing since 2004 have features of equivalence. Admittedly, after paying these fees, an entrepreneur may legally invest in Polish maritime areas, but the amount of the fee refers to the value of these investments—not to the value of the mutual benefit of the public administration body.

Doubts also arose in response to a statement included in the same justification of the draft law on offshore wind farms, which reads as follows[26]:

> The fee is an equivalent benefit and in this context it should be noted that the amount of the additional fee within the concession fee for the producers from offshore wind farms is adequate and takes into account the costs incurred by numerous bodies performing tasks related to the development of offshore wind farms in Poland.

When determining the amount of the fee for offshore wind farms, the authors of the draft referred—as indicated earlier in Sect. 8.2.—to a hypothetical real estate tax value. At the same time, they declared that the value of the concession fee corresponds

[24] https://legislacja.gov.pl/projekt/12329105/katalog/12656009#12656009, retrieved 15 April 2021.

[25] The maximum rate provided for by the L.T.C.A. is 2% of the tax base.

[26] https://www.sejm.gov.pl/Sejm9.nsf/PrzebiegProc.xsp?id=0282D90367CB9DADC1258637003 0F731, retrieved 15 April 2021.

to the costs of public administration activities. Therefore, this case reflects a benefit that has been discussed in the literature, which disguised a tax as a 'fee' (Antonów, 2017, pp. 487–496).

The legislators' solution may entail specific negative consequences, including even the risk of declaring the legal regulation of concession fees unconstitutional. The Polish Constitution sets very strict requirements for tax regulation. According to Article 217 of the constitution, 'The imposition of taxes, other public tributes, the determination of entities, subjects of taxation and tax rates, as well as the principles of granting reliefs and remissions and categories of entities exempted from taxes shall be made by means of a law'. Therefore, it explicitly states that tax rates must be provided for in the law while, for fees, no such requirement is included. Meanwhile, the rate of the concession fee for offshore wind farms results from an ordinance of the Council of Ministers and not from an act. The Energy Law only includes the maximum rate of the coefficient which is used to calculate the concession fee. Therefore, the Polish Constitution was likely violated.

The situation would differ slightly if the local character of this tax (called a 'concession fee') were maintained. In relation to local taxes and fees, Article 168 of the Constitution of the Republic of Poland would apply, according to which, 'Local government units have the right to establish the amount of local taxes and fees within the scope specified in the act'. In practice, in Poland, Parliament determines by law only the maximum rates of local taxes and fees, and specific rates applicable in a given municipality are adopted by a municipal council. Therefore, if a concession fee had a local character and were collected by the relevant municipality, the council of this municipality could prescribe the rates of this fee as long as they did not exceed the maximum rate set by law. However, the constitution does not afford such freedom to government bodies.

8.5 Alternative Approaches to Taxing Offshore Wind Farms

It should be considered if better solutions were available to Polish legislators in order to close the loophole that allowed offshore wind farms to avoid taxation.

A potential solution was the introduction of appropriate amendments to the provisions of L.T.C.A. or the Tax Ordinance, which would define the responsibility of a municipal council when local jurisdiction cannot be established according to general rules. Similar to the case of determining the responsibility of the tax authority without local jurisdiction as the President of the Capital City of Warsaw, the council of the municipality responsible for determining tax rates for objects in the Exclusive Economic Zone could be deemed the council of the Capital City of Warsaw. Such a solution could raise doubts about its compliance with the constitution. In Poland, a resolution of a municipal council is an act of local law. However, in line with Article 87, Clause 2, of the Polish Constitution, local law acts constitute a source of law exclusively within the area in which the given municipal council operates, and the Polish Exclusive Economic Zone—as an area that does not constitute the territory of Poland—is not an area where the council of the Capital City of Warsaw (or any other municipal council) operates. Additionally, a tax authority other than the tax authority of the Municipality of Warsaw would operate on the basis of such an act of local law. Thus, one municipality would decide the revenue levels of other municipalities.

Another possible solution could be the introduction of a provision specifying the tax rate applicable to structures in the Polish Exclusive Economic Zone directly into the L.T.C.A. (i.e. without needing to refer to the resolution of the municipal council). In such a case, the tax would—as an exception—be calculated based on the statutory rate. However, the authority responsible for collecting the tax would be the President of the Capital City of Warsaw, and the capital would generate income on this account. This solution could, however, raise doubts about systemic compatibility; the real estate tax is a local tax, so the responsibility for determining its amount lies with local government units, following directly from the constitution.[27] Admittedly, the constitution stipulates that these units have such authority only 'to the extent specified in the Act', but so far, legislators have always granted local governments such authority in relation to taxes that they themselves collect. The solution granting tax revenues to Warsaw (and not, for example, coastal municipalities) could be accused of favouring the capital city. Another option would be adopting a legal fiction that the Exclusive Economic Zone is nevertheless an area of the coastal municipalities. Even if legal doubts were to be disregarded, such a solution would always give rise to practical problems related to tax assessment.

[27] Article 168 of the Polish Constitution: 'Local self-government units shall have the right to determine the amount of local taxes and charges to the extent determined by law'.

Chapter 9
The Taxation of Assets Used for Energy Storage

Abstract In the field of energy storage, drawing conclusions about whether conventional energy is preferential to renewable energy from a tax perspective, or vice versa, is difficult. Notably, while electrochemical storage facilities are mainly used by wind and photovoltaic power plants, conventional pumped storage plants are used for both types of power generation. Moreover, the tax rules favour, to some extent, electrochemical storage, whose value comprises almost entirely non-construction (and non-taxable) components. Pumped storage plants, on the other hand, are groups of significantly smaller facilities which, in addition to technical equipment, include a number of construction objects, subjecting them to the real estate tax to a much greater extent.

Keywords Energy storage · Electrochemical storage · Pumped storage power plants

9.1 Introduction

Energy storage facilities are an important component of a country's energy system, allowing the storage of surplus generated energy that the transmission grid cannot absorb at a given moment. This function is needed for any type of power plant to produce energy. In the case of conventional power plants, energy storage allows for the accumulation of surplus energy produced at times of lower demand (e.g. at night). Energy storage is also particularly important for renewable energy sources (wind power plants and photovoltaics), which produce highly fluctuating amounts of energy due to weather factors.

Linking a power plant to an energy storage facility increases its energy efficiency. At the same time, energy storage facilities constitute high-cost infrastructure, the taxation of which through the real estate tax may reduce investments' profitability. For this reason, the problem of taxing energy storage facilities with the real estate tax requires separate analysis.

Pursuant to the legal definition contained in Polish regulations, an 'electric energy storage facility' is understood as an installation that enables the storage of electric

W. Morawski and A. Kałążny, *The Taxation of Energy-Sector Assets: Polish Tax Legislation on the Eve of Energy Transformation*, SpringerBriefs in Energy,
https://doi.org/10.1007/978-3-031-15673-1_9

energy and its injection into the power grid.[1] Among the types of energy storage, one can distinguish *mechanical storage* (e.g. in pumped storage power plants), thermal storage (featuring heat accumulation) or electrochemical storage (consisting of rechargeable batteries or accumulators). The following analysis covers electrochemical storage (based on batteries) and pumped storage as the two most common types of energy storage in Poland.

9.2 Electrochemical Storage

Electrochemical energy storage (based on batteries) is currently the most commonly used solution to accompany renewable energy power plants (wind and photovoltaic power plants). Their advantage is their ability to be located anywhere and their relatively small size, which is an important benefit in the case of highly distributed renewable energy.

From a technical perspective, energy storage units are battery banks located in either a special enclosure (usually a metal cabinet) to protect them from external factors or a dedicated building directly. They collect the surplus energy produced by a photovoltaic or wind turbine installation, accumulate it and then transfer it to the electricity grid to which they are connected. From a functional point of view, energy storage is not a necessary component of the proper energy production installation operation. However, as already mentioned, their connection to such an installation increases its efficiency by reducing the losses associated with the production of surplus energy that cannot be fed into the grid at any given moment.

Precisely because of the function that an energy storage facility performs, from the perspective of the regulations governing the real estate tax (and the related provisions of the C.L.A.), such a facility does not constitute a structure subject to the real estate tax. For the energy storage to be considered a construction device (taxed as a structure) or an installation constituting an element of a construction object in the form of a structure (in accordance with the definition of a 'construction object'[2]), energy storage would need to ensure the possibility of using the structure in accordance with its designation. However, an energy storage facility does not ensure the possibility of using a power plant for its intended purpose since it can function properly without doing so. Moreover, a power plant is not a construction object in itself; only certain elements that make up the power plant as a whole, such as the foundations for equipment, support structures, cable lines and buildings, can be regarded as construction objects. In order to classify an energy storage facility as a construction device, it

[1] Article 2, Point 17, of the Act of 20 February 2015 on renewable energy sources (Journal of Laws of 2021, Item 610, as amended) in connection with Article 3(10k) of the Act of 10 April 1997—Energy Law (Journal of Laws 2021, Item 716, as amended).

[2] According to Article 3(1) of the C.L.A., a 'construction object' is a building, a structure or a small architectural object, including installations that ensure the possibility of using an object in accordance with its intended purpose, erected using construction materials.

would have to be demonstrated to enable the use of these construction objects for their intended purposes, a functional connection that does not exist.

The subject of energy storage facilities' treatment from a real estate tax perspective has not been addressed in the jurisprudence to date. However, in this context, the judgements of the Supreme Administrative Court that consider transformers, distribution equipment and battery banks to be part of the power network—and, consequently, taxable structures—must be considered.[3] According to the Supreme Administrative Court, the argument in favour of such a tax qualification for said equipment is the fact that they are an indispensable part of the electricity network and that their removal would prevent the supply of electricity to consumers. However, this argument does not apply to energy storage facilities, which are the ancillary infrastructure of a power plant, because—as we have indicated—both the power plant itself and the electricity grid to which it is connected can function perfectly well without storage facilities.

Only the construction portions of electrochemical storage facilities may be subject to the real estate tax. For batteries located in dedicated buildings, the subject of taxation is—obviously—the buildings whose taxable base constitutes their usable area. However, for energy storage facilities located in their own enclosures and sited outside buildings, the subject of taxation may be particularly the foundations on which they are placed, which are taxed as structures on the basis of their value. In both cases, the vast majority of an energy storage facility's value, attributable to its technical components, is beyond the scope of taxation.

9.3 Pumped Storage Power Plants

Pumped storage plants are the oldest and most common type of energy storage in the world. They are characterised by large capacity and high efficiency. Their characteristic feature is their need for different levels between two reservoirs used to transfer water stored in the power plant. This requirement means that pumped storage plants can generally only be located in geographically suitable areas. Unlike electrochemical storage, they do not form a dispersed network of small installations in the immediate vicinity of generating installations. Pumped storage plants are relatively few and large facilities to which surplus energy is transferred via transmission lines, often from power plants located far away.

This difference in the characteristics of both types of energy storage (pumped storage and electrochemical storage) translates into their completely different construction—which, in turn, may entail different tax treatments. In a simplification suitable for tax analysis, a pumped storage plant can be said to comprise lower and upper reservoirs, a pipeline that transfers water between these reservoirs and a pump-turbine that pushes water to the upper reservoir and generates energy using

[3] Supreme Administrative Court judgement of 22 July 2020, II FSK 1064/20; Supreme Administrative Court judgement of 24 November 2020, II FSK 1317/20.

water released into the lower reservoir. A pumped storage plant may also include associated facilities, such as buildings.

The artificial or natural reservoirs that make up a pumped storage power plant do not in themselves constitute structures. Instead, they occupy large areas that potentially generate land tax. However, this tax is not a material burden because legislators have provided for a preferential real estate tax rate for land underlying surface waters or the flowing surface waters of lakes and artificial reservoirs (Article 5[1][1][b] of the L.T.C.A.), and this rate is approximately 1000 times lower than the rate for other land associated with economic activity.

The object of real estate taxation for pumped storage power plants will certainly be the pipeline that transfers water between reservoirs, which is included in the definition of a 'linear object' (Article 3, Item 3a of the C.L.A.) and is, in turn, indicated as an example of a 'structure' in Article 3, Item 3, of the C.L.A. The foundations for power equipment included in a pumped storage power plant will also qualify as 'taxable structures'.

On the other hand, a pump-turbine itself does not constitute a 'construction object' or, consequently, the subject of the real estate tax. We should point out that, as in the case of batteries that form part of an electrochemical storage facility, the pump-turbine cannot be classified as a 'construction device' because it does not ensure the intended use of any construction object. In particular, the electricity grid does not require a pumped storage plant for its operation; it can only be considered a valuable addition to the grid, allowing the storage of surplus energy that would otherwise be lost.

The hydrotechnical structures included in a pumped storage power plant (indicated as an example of a structure in Article 3[3] of the C.L.A.) may be subject to the real estate tax. This term does not have a legal definition in the L.T.C.A., but it is defined in the Regulation of the Minister of Environment of 20 April 2007 on the technical conditions necessary for hydrotechnical structures and their location. In accordance with Paragraph 3(1) of this regulation, a 'hydrotechnical structure' is a structure that includes related technical equipment and installations and is used for water management and shaping and using water resources, including—inter alia—earth and concrete dams and the basins of water reservoirs, together with slopes and escarpments, canals or hydro-engineering pipelines. All these elements may be present in the construction of a pumped storage power plant and, at the same time, constitute taxable structures. Interestingly, the provision also mentions hydroelectric power plants and pumping stations as 'hydrotechnical structures'. Does the entire pumped storage power plant (as a special type of hydroelectric power plant), together with its pump-turbine, constitute a taxable structure? The answer to this question should be negative because the definition of a 'structure' in the C.L.A. (to which the L.T.C.A. refers directly) unambiguously indicates that only the construction parts of technical equipment qualify as structures. Extending the scope of the real estate tax to technical equipment based on the provisions of this regulation would, in this case, infringe upon the constitutional principle that the subject of taxation must be determined exclusively by means of an act (Kosikowski, 1999, p. 8).

Chapter 10
The Taxation of Transmission Lines and Facilities: A History of Unexpected Regulatory Changes and Unstable Jurisprudence

Abstract The issue concerning the property used to transmit electricity illustrates the unstable and largely unpredictable approach of Polish legislators and administrative courts to the real estate tax on energy infrastructure. Over the last quarter of a century, the situation has changed dramatically—from the tax exemption of transmission lines to their taxation and, finally (according to the latest position of the Supreme Administrative Court), to the taxation of the entire power grid with its associated equipment, such as transformers. The only positive gesture that legislators have made towards transmission operators are the changes described in this chapter concerning the taxation of the land under transmission lines. The surprising broadening of the scope for real estate taxation that we have described applies equally to conventional and renewable energy since both these branches use the transmission infrastructure equally. For conventional power generation, the backbone of the transmission network is, in principle, already in place, but it requires major upgrades over the coming years. For renewable energy sources, however, the creation of completely new sections of transmission lines is necessary to receive the electricity generated from power plants and distribute it around the country. In both cases, investments will increase the real estate tax base. Each extension to the definition of 'structures' in order to include the technical equipment connected to the power grid significantly increases grid maintenance costs.

Keywords Transmission lines · Transformer stations · Transformers

10.1 Transmission Lines

As a rule, power lines constitute structures for the purposes of the real estate tax. The definition of 'structure' in Article 3(3) of the C.L.A. indicates, inter alia, linear objects as examples. Pursuant to the definition provided in Article 3(3a) of the C.L.A.,

---

The chapter is, inter alia, the result of research carried out under the grant funded by the National Science Centre (Poland), No. 2019/35/B/HS5/00554, 'Interpretation of tax law in the context of passing time'.

W. Morawski and A. Kałążny, *The Taxation of Energy-Sector Assets: Polish Tax Legislation on the Eve of Energy Transformation*, SpringerBriefs in Energy,
https://doi.org/10.1007/978-3-031-15673-1_10

a 'linear object' includes, inter alia, power lines and traction. Therefore, as examples of structures literally indicated in the provisions of the C.L.A., power lines are subject to the real estate tax.

We should point out that, according to Article 7, Item 1, Point 5 of the L.T.C.A. in its initial wording (in force since the act's entry into force; Journal of Laws 1991, No. 9, Item 31), power lines, for example, were exempted from the real estate tax. Then, since 1 January 1997, real estate tax exemption was applicable to, inter alia, the transmission and distribution power lines (*Journal of Laws* 1996, No. 91, Item 409). This exemption was fully eliminated as of 1 January 2001 by virtue of the Act of 13 October 2000 (Dz. U. No. 95, Item 1041) on amendments to the act on the revenues of local government units in 1999 and 2000 and certain other acts, which were motivated by the desire to increase municipalities' budgetary revenues (Kałążny, 2020, p. 155).

The jurisprudence expressed the opinion that, in order to classify power cables as 'structures', they must be connected to an object that constitutes a 'structure' on the grounds of the C.L.A. In particular, in disputes concerning the taxation of objects that constitute a wind power plant argued that connected power cables do not constitute taxable structures because they do not form a technical or utilitarian whole with structures (towers and foundations) but are connected to technical equipment (a turbine) which does not constitute taxable structures. This position was accepted, for example, in the judgements of the Provincial Administrative Court in Poznań of 9 November 2011.[1] Importantly, however, these judgements were issued in a legal state in which the C.L.A. did not explicitly indicate a 'power line' or 'traction' in defining a 'linear object'.

As the L.T.C.A. currently stands, energy infrastructure—including transmission lines—does not benefit from statutory exemptions or exclusions and is taxed under the general rules like other business-related structures.

10.2 Transformer Stations

The element of energy infrastructure which has aroused the most controversy in recent few years in the context of real estate taxation is transformers (and other energy equipment included in transformer stations).

Transformers are technical devices used to transfer alternating currents from one electrical circuit to another, usually with a simultaneous change in electrical voltage. Due to their function, they can be an important part of the energy transmission network (appearing at the junction of the high-voltage network and the medium-voltage network), but they also serve end consumers (changing from high or medium voltage to low voltage). Therefore, from a functional perspective, transformers can be divided into those that ensure the use of the transmission network for their intended purpose (which are usually the property of transmission entrepreneurs) and those

[1] III Sa/Po 495/11; III Sa/Po 534/11; III Sa/Po 491/11; III Sa/Po 549/11.

without which the transmission network can function but which are necessary for end customers to use the current from the network to power their equipment (transformers of the latter type are often not the property of transmission entrepreneurs but belong to entrepreneurs, who use them to supply their machines with electricity). This division is important for real estate tax treatment.

The second criterion for the division of transformers is the manner of their assembly. From the real estate tax perspective, transformers can be divided into two basic groups based on the criterion of whether the construction element to which the technical equipment (a transformer) is connected is a building or a structure (Morawski, 2013, pp. 147–155):

1. transformers located in buildings and
2. transformers located outside buildings.

10.2.1 Substation Facilities' Tax Classification

For transformers located in buildings, the disputed issue was the tax treatment of the transformer station itself—that is, whether it were a building or a structure on account of its function. Importantly, the taxation of transformer stations as structures, treating their full value as the basis for taxation (including the value of the building, together with the equipment located in it) is many times less advantageous for taxpayers than taxing these stations as buildings based of their usable area.

The jurisprudence expressed a view according to which construction objects that fulfil the conditions for treatment as buildings (having all the characteristics of a 'building' specified in Article 1a.(1.1.1) of the L.T.C.A.—that is, a permanent connection to the ground, a foundation, and a separate space by means of building partitions and roof), were treated from the perspective of the real estate tax as structures because they were filled, to a significant extent, with power devices. This position was first expressed by the Supreme Administrative Court in its judgements of 1 January 2008,[2] in which the court agreed with the tax authorities' recognising transformer stations with the features of buildings as 'structures' taxed on their value, based—inter alia—on the following reasoning:

> A transformer station together with power distribution boards, on the other hand, is not a place of human work, a storehouse, warehouse or other premises where human needs are realised. Instead, it is an integral part of the electricity network. According to the tax authorities, distribution transformer stations fulfil the same function as pole transformer stations.

In the Supreme Administrative Court's opinion, the classification of a construction object as a 'building' or a 'structure' for the purposes of settlements vis-à-vis the real estate tax should be determined not only by its construction but also by its function. This concept contradicted not only the previous approach of the administrative courts but also the doctrine (Etel & Teszner, 2006, pp. 22–58). and the Ministry of Finance.

---

[2] II FSK 1309/07; II FSK 1310/07; II FSK 1311/07; II FSK 1312/07; II FSK 1313/07.

This ministry, in its letter LK-727/MM/03 of 15 May 2003 by the Director of the Local Tax and Cadastre Department, indicated that installations inside a building (e.g. a water supply, a sewage system, an electrical system, a computer system, a telephone system and cable television) are part of a building and not subject to separate taxation because a building's taxable base is its usable area. This position was consolidated in a number of judgements issued later.[3] In the courts' view, if a construction object (transformer station) 'exceeds the statutory features of a building' (i.e. is permanently connected to the ground, separated from the surrounding space by means of building partitions, has a foundation and a roof and, at the same time, is 'cubature-filled with equipment'), it may be regarded as a structure on the grounds of the L.T.C.A.

This position was criticised by representatives of the doctrine, who pointed out that—in accordance with the legal definitions of the terms 'building' and 'structure'—only an object which does not have the features of a building can be classified as a structure. (In accordance with the definition of a 'structure' set out in Article 1a(1)(2) of the L.T.C.A., a 'structure' is understood in particular as a construction object within the meaning of the provisions of the C.L.A. which is not a 'building' (Popławski, 2015, pp. 4–7).)

An interpretation of the L.T.C.A. provisions favourable to taxpayers was adopted by the Constitutional Court in its judgement of 13 December 2017,[4] according to which the administrative courts' interpretation of the provisions of the L.T.C.A. allowing for the recognition as a 'structure' of an object that fulfils the features of a building is inconsistent with the constitution because it adds to the definition of the 'object of real estate taxation criteria' (being filled with equipment and having a specific function) elements that were not included by legislators in the L.T.C.A (Dowgier, 2018, pp. 33–40). This approach was consolidated in the resolution of a panel of seven judges of the Supreme Administrative Court of 29 September 2021.[5] This resolution confirmed that the function or purpose of a building cannot change its tax classification as a structure.

A transformer station facility may be a structure if it does not have at least one of the features listed in the definition of a 'building' (e.g. it is not permanently attached to the ground or does not have a foundation) (Pahl, 2009, pp. 9–14). This situation sometimes occurs in the case of small, prefabricated container stations.

At the same time, the doctrine has also expressed the opinion that, for example, a gas pressure regulating and measurement station cannot be treated in isolation from the rest of its network because they form a functional whole, which may lead to the entire network's (including technical elements) taxation as a structure (Pahl, 2019).

---

[3] E.g. the Provincial Administrative Court in Kraków judgement of 19 November 2015, I SA/Kr 998/15, in relation to a container transformer station; judgement of the Supreme Administrative Court of 26 February 2015, II FSK 65/13, in relation to a container mobile phone base station; judgement of the Supreme Administrative Court of 27 March 2017, II FSK 311/15, in relation to gas reduction stations.

[4] SK 48/15.

[5] III FPS 1/21.

10.2.2 *The Tax Treatment of Transformers Located in Buildings*

Recognising a transformer station as a building does not preclude disputes over the taxation of the transformers located therein. The jurisprudence of the administrative courts expresses the view that transformers located inside buildings constitute separately taxed structures because they are a so-called technical and utilitarian whole with the power grid, which is a structure.[6] A parallel position was presented by some representatives of the doctrine (Popławski, 2015, p. 15), based on a broader concept of a structure located in a building. According to this position, the location of a given object inside a building does not automatically mean that the object cannot constitute a structure subject to the real estate tax on its value (Etel, n.d.). In the jurisprudence, this issue does not seem to be clearly resolved. According to some judgements, power equipment located in a transformer station—such as transformers, technical equipment, telemechanics, suppression reactors, power supplies and batteries—is not a technical network (structure) simply because it is connected to the power grid.[7]

Recently, in the Supreme Administrative Court jurisprudence, a position has again been presented according to which transformers, distribution equipment and battery banks are considered part of the power network and, consequently, taxable structures. According to the Supreme Administrative Court, the argument favouring such a tax classification for said equipment is the fact that it constitutes an indispensable part of the power network and that its removal would make supplying electricity to consumers impossible.[8] Seemingly, this position should certainly not be applied to transformers that change a medium voltage to a low voltage, which ensures the use of technical devices that draw electricity from the network for their intended purposes and not the power network as such, which does not require the connection of such transformers to function. For transformers that belong to transmission entrepreneurs and operate between high- and medium-voltage networks, the reasoning presented in the cited judgements of the Supreme Administrative Court may, seemingly, apply. However, we should point out that the rule is to tax only such objects that are explicitly indicated in the C.L.A. regulations as structures. In the case of technical equipment, the definition of a 'structure' in Article 3(3) of the C.L.A. unequivocally indicates that only its construction parts (e.g. a pole) or foundations constitute a structure. A possible treatment of technical devices as objects covered by the C.L.A. regulation is provided by the definition of a 'construction device' (C.L.A., Article 3, Item 9). However, the jurisprudence and doctrine emphasise that a technical device can only constitute a taxable structure as a construction device if the type of technical device is explicitly indicated in the definition of a 'construction device' (Kałążny, 2020,

---

[6] E.g. the Supreme Administrative Court judgement of 2 February 2010, II FSK 1024/08.

[7] E.g. the Provincial Administrative Court in Kielce judgement of 20 April 2017, I SA/Ke 118/17; the Provincial Administrative Court in Kielce judgement of 18 May 2017, I SA/Ke 119/17; the Provincial Administrative Court in Olsztyn judgement of 28 June 2017, I SA/Ol 302/17.

[8] Supreme Administrative Court judgement of 22 July 2020, II FSK 1064/20; Supreme Administrative Court judgement of 24 November 2020, II FSK 1317/20.

pp. 11–16). Yet, transformers are not mentioned by name in Article 3.9 of the C.L.A. In the current authors' opinion, therefore, the taxation of transformers as structures is not supported by the provisions of the law in force. The taxation of all devices connected to a power network, based on the argument that the network needs them to function properly, would lead to absurd conclusions requiring the taxation of not only transformers but also—for example—the computers that control the network (Morawski, 2013, pp. 147–155).

10.2.2.1 The Tax Treatment of Transformers Located Outside Buildings

In the case of transformers located outside buildings, whether—on the grounds of the L.T.C.A.—the equipment located on power poles or on foundations constitutes a structure (as an element of the power network) or whether it constitutes technical equipment that is not subject to the real estate tax must be determined. In both cases, in principle, a pole (as a construction part) or a foundation on which a transformer is placed is, doubtless, a taxable structure. According to the unfavourable approach for taxpayers, transformers located on poles or foundations (similar to those located in buildings) form a technical and utilitarian whole with the power network, which supports their treatment as an element of a taxable structure.[9] At the same time, the jurisprudence also presented a view according to which transformers placed on poles or foundations do not constitute structures subject to the real estate tax.[10]

The line of jurisprudence favourable to taxpayers has been consolidated by a series of judgements by the Supreme Administrative Court on 7 July 2015.[11] These judgements indicated that, in order to qualify a given object as a 'structure', the specific category listed in the definition of a 'structure' in Article 3(3) of the C.L.A. to which the object belongs must be indicated; thus, a transformer that constitutes electrical power equipment is not, in any way, similar to the example structures presented in the act. Consequently, only a pole or a foundation should be subject to the real estate tax (as a constructional portion of a technical device or a foundation for a technical device—structure categories indicated directly in the C.L.A. definition of 'structures').

For a long time, the establishment of such a line of jurisprudence seemed to close the discussion on the real estate taxation of transformer equipment itself. However, the latest Supreme Administrative Court jurisprudence (cited in the previous section) treating power equipment as a taxable element of a structure in the form of a power

[9] E.g. the Supreme Administrative Court judgement of 2 February 2010, II FSK 1024/08; the Provincial Administrative Court in Łódź judgement of 27 February 2008, I SA/Wr 1783/07.

[10] E.g. the Supreme Administrative Court judgement of 27 September 2013, II FSK 2493/12; the Provincial Administrative Court in Gliwice judgement of 28 February 2011, I SA/Gl 1362/10; the Provincial Administrative Court in Wrocław judgement of 21 July 2008, I SA/Wr 460/08; the Provincial Administrative Court in Gdańsk judgement of 21 December 2011, I SA/Gd 1092/11; the Provincial Administrative Court in Łódź judgement of 18 December 2013, I SA/Łd 1340/13.

[11] II FSK 3184/13; II FSK 1672/13; II FSK 1552/13.

grid seems to have reopened disputes between taxpayers and tax authorities. We should point out that the change in the Supreme Administrative Court's approach is surprising insofar as no changes to the provisions governing real estate taxation in recent years would justify a radical change in the approach to the possible taxation of transformers (and other power equipment). Consequently, the unexpected change in the court's position may adversely affect the business planning of entrepreneurs who own such equipment. This issue concerns many different industries (transformers are, for example, among the equipment of most manufacturing plants or logistics centres). But, above all, it may negatively influence the power industry. The Polish electricity transmission grid requires significant investments in the coming years, and the administrative courts' unpredictable position on taxing this grid's most valuable elements increases the uncertainty concerning the amount of future tax that will be levied.

10.3 The Land Under Transmission Lines

The key issue related to the taxation of the land over (or under) which electric transmission lines run is whether such land is occupied and connected with business activity. The notions of land's 'occupation' and 'connection' to business activity are key for the Polish real estate tax because, as a rule, they determine whether land is subject to the real estate tax and at what rate. (For more detail, see Chap. 7: 'The Taxation of Land Used for Energy Production').

We should point out that transmission lines run over significant areas of agricultural land, forests or wasteland, which are subject to the real estate tax only if they are considered occupied for the purpose of conducting business activities. Otherwise, they may be excluded or exempted from taxation. This problem has been subjected to long-standing disputes between taxpayers (transmission entrepreneurs) and tax authorities.

Since 2016, the prevailing view in the jurisprudence has suggested that the land under power lines is occupied to conduct transmission entrepreneurs' business activities.[12] This view has been controversial to the extent that the manifestation of this activity has been, for many commentators, at least debatable. In the courts' opinion, the land under transmission lines is occupied for business activity because, based on entrepreneurs' rights under the transmission easement established on the land or relevant agreements concluded with the landowner, they could obtain unlimited access to the land. This right manifests, for example, in the entry of employees performing maintenance work or removing defects from the land. Taxpayers who have defended the thesis that such land is not used for business activity emphasised that, in principle, the land under transmission lines is used for agricultural or forestry activities without any restrictions, so it cannot be said to be used for business activity (recall that agricultural and forestry activities do not constitute business activity).

[12] Judgement of the Supreme Administrative Court of 9 June 2016, II FSK 1156/14.

This position, however, was not recognised by the courts, which argued that the fact of carrying out agricultural or forestry activities at the same time does not exclude the land's occupation for business activity.

Courtroom failures have motivated taxpayers to take action to promote legislative changes. The introduction, effective from 1 January 2019, of a new provision referring directly to 'transmission infrastructure' should certainly be considered a success for transmission entrepreneurs in this field. Pursuant to Article 1a(2a)(4) of the L.T.C.A., the land occupied for transmission facilities that form part of an enterprise which is engaged in telecommunications activities, activities transmitting or distributing liquids, steam, gases or electricity or engaged in the transport of extracted natural gas or crude oil (as well as the land occupied for technological belts and protective zones in the vicinity of such facilities) shall not be deemed to be connected with the conduct of business activities. Yet, this exclusion does not apply to land held by a transmission entrepreneur in their own right, perpetual usufruct or ownership; therefore, it applies primarily to forests and agricultural land owned by other entities.

The fact that the land under transmission lines is not associated with business activity, a view which has resulted directly from the L.T.C.A. provision, means that this land cannot be subject to the maximum real estate tax rate. However, one may doubt the content of this provision which indicates that the land in question is not associated with business activity; for instance, one might ask whether, in that case, it cannot be occupied for that activity.

The notion of 'occupation for economic activity', despite playing a key role in land taxation via the real estate tax, lacks a legal definition in the L.T.C.A. regulations. The doctrine uniformly accepts that land occupied for business activity should be understood as land that is actually used for business activity (Borszowski, n.d.), a position which the jurisprudence of administrative courts does not doubt.[13]

On the contrary, the notion of 'connection with economic activity' is legally defined in Article 1a(1)(3) of the L.T.C.A., according to which land, buildings and structures held by an entrepreneur or another entity conducting business activity are deemed to be connected with the performance of business activity. Therefore, the doctrine generally accepts that land 'connected with business activity' is a broader concept than 'occupation for the purpose of conducting business activity' because establishing actual operations on the land is not necessary, merely the fact of the entrepreneur's possession of the land (Drofiszyn & Warzel, 2020, pp. 14–16). However, this position has become outdated, to some extent, in connection with the verdict of the Constitutional Tribunal of 24 February 2021.[14] This judgement found Article 1a, Section 1.3, of the L.T.C.A. to be unconstitutional to the extent that it makes the classification of land, buildings and structures that are subject to the real estate tax as land, buildings and structures connected with pursuing business activity (resulting in the obligation to pay the real estate tax at a higher rate) depend exclusively on the entrepreneur's ownership. In the judgement's justification, the Constitutional Tribunal indicated that the fact that land is associated with

[13] E.g. judgement of the Supreme Administrative Court of 11 May 2010, II FSK 2181/2008.

[14] SK 39/19.

the performance of business activity should be determined not only by its possession by an entrepreneur but also by other factual circumstances which indicate that the entrepreneur actually uses the land for the conducted business activity.

This judgement of the Constitutional Tribunal aimed to equate the notions of 'connection' and 'occupation' for business purposes. In the context of the land under transmission lines—which, according to the current legislation, is not associated with business activity—whether the lack of such an association automatically means a lack of occupation for business activity remains to be decided. At this point, the resolution of a panel of seven judges of the Supreme Administrative Court of 9 December 2019[15] is worth citing. The court addressed the problem of determining the real estate taxpayer in the case of transmission lines that ran over land which belonged to State Forests. The resolution noted,

> The fact that forest land on which a transmission easement has been established is not at the same time in the possession of an entrepreneur or other entity conducting business activities [...] does not mean, therefore, that it is not occupied for business activities. Indeed, the possession of land is not a prerequisite for determining whether land is occupied for the conduct of business activities.

Thus, the Supreme Administrative Court allows for the possibility that land unrelated to business activity may be occupied for business activity. In the case concerning the resolution, the Supreme Administrative Court held that the land under the lines on which the transmission easement was established was not possessed by the transmission entrepreneur; therefore, in accordance with the provisions of the L.T.C.A., it was deemed unrelated to the entrepreneur's business activity. (Recall that this resolution concerned the legal status prior to 1 January 2019 and prior to the issuance of the aforementioned Constitutional Tribunal judgement SK 39/19.) At the same time, the Supreme Administrative Court did not exclude the possibility that the transmission entrepreneur may perform actual activities on the land which would lead to its occupation for business activities. Seemingly, under the law's current status, such a situation should not occur; if legislators considered that actions undertaken by a transmission entrepreneur do not lead to associating the land with their business activity, this conclusion may be extended to suggest that the actions do not lead to occupation either. Nevertheless, importantly, the legislative change—which was intended to release agricultural and forest land over which transmission lines run from real estate taxation—was insufficiently precise. In the current authors' opinion, to eliminate doubts as to the tax treatment of such land, the L.T.C.A. should provide that such land is not associated with or occupied for the transmission entrepreneur's business activity.

[15] II FPS 3/19.

Chapter 11
Allocation of Tax Revenue Between State and Local Government Units

Abstract The energy transition away from coal-fired power generation shifts tax revenues between municipalities. These revenues are more dispersed than in the case of the taxation of coal-based energy. In addition, renewable energy can develop better in hitherto poorer regions, especially those that have so far not been attractive for settlement and agriculture.

Keywords Energy transition · Asset taxation · Local taxes · Tax police

11.1 Introduction

Wealth taxes are local taxes in Poland. This is expressed in the fact that property tax, agricultural tax and forestry tax are levied by the tax authorities of municipalities, it is the municipalities that set the amount (within the limits set by legal acts) and these taxes constitute the entire revenue of municipalities.

Such a solution implements the provisions of the Constitution of the Republic of Poland. In accordance with Article 167 of the Polish Constitution, territorial self-government units shall be guaranteed a share in public revenues in accordance with the tasks assigned to them. The Constitution defines that the revenues of local government units are their own revenues as well as general subventions and purpose-specific subsidies from the state budget.[1] These are rather laconic formulations, which do not determine what public revenues the communes receive. In accordance with Article 167(3) of the Polish Constitution, the sources of revenues of local government units are specified by statute. This law is currently the Act of 13 November 2003 on revenues of local government units.[2] In accordance with Article 3(1) of this Act, the revenues of local government units are their own revenues, general subvention and purpose-specific subsidies from the state budget. In addition, within the meaning of the Act, the revenues of local government units are also the shares in revenues from income tax from natural persons and income tax from legal persons. In addition,

[1] Article 167(2) of the Polish Constitution.

[2] Consolidated text: Official Journal of 2018, it. 1530, as amended.

W. Morawski and A. Kałążny, *The Taxation of Energy-Sector Assets: Polish Tax Legislation on the Eve of Energy Transformation*, SpringerBriefs in Energy,
https://doi.org/10.1007/978-3-031-15673-1_11

revenues of local government units may be e.g. non-returnable funds from foreign sources, funds from the budget of the European Union or other funds specified in separate regulations.

Own revenues of municipalities are mainly taxes and fees. Some are collected for the benefit of municipalities by state tax authorities. These are certain forms of income tax, tax on civil law transactions, tax on inheritance and donations, and stamp duty. However, of key importance is the real estate tax (to a lesser extent also the agricultural and forestry taxes as taxes complementary to the real estate tax), which the municipality collects on its own through the activity of its own tax authority. From the point of view of the subject of the study, it is important to note that the municipalities are also entitled to a part of the revenue from the exploitation fee, which is collected from entities extracting natural resources from underground. According to Article 141 G.M.L.A., municipalities are generally entitled to 60% of mining fee revenues. In the case of hydrocarbon production royalties, 60% of the royalty is the revenue of the municipality, 15% is the revenue of the county (a higher-level local government unit, usually comprising several municipalities), and 15% is the revenue of the province (Poland is divided into 16 provinces) in which the mining operations are conducted. If the activity is conducted in the territory of more than one municipality, one powiat or one province, fees constitute their revenue in proportion to the size of the area covered by the activity or the amount of extracted mineral or the amount of substances, waste or carbon dioxide put into the rock mass.[3]

It is worth mentioning that municipalities also receive a share of state taxes. The share of personal income tax revenue from taxpayers residing in the municipality is 39.34%, and the share of corporate income tax revenue from taxpayers based in the municipality is 6.71%.

The solution of allocating property tax revenues to municipalities is typical of modern states (if they allocate any taxes to municipalities for self-administration at all). Property taxes such as property tax, agricultural tax and forestry tax are characterised by low mobility of the tax object, which facilitates their collection and minimises the risk of disputes (More on this topic, among others: Fjeldstad (2001, pp. 5–7), Kowalik (2012, pp. 103–113), Shah (2014).

11.2 Distribution of Wealth Tax Revenues Between Municipalities—Standard Solutions

Regulation allocating revenue from certain taxes to municipalities is a prelude to the fundamental issue of how to distribute this revenue to individual municipalities.

[3] Article 141(3) G.M.L.A.

In the case of land taxation, there is no problem with this. The tax is simply collected by the municipality where the land is located.[4] The same is true for buildings.[5] Theoretically, there could be a building located on the border of municipalities, but this is an extremely rare case.

The real problem arises when it comes to buildings. They are usually quite complex and sometimes extend for many kilometres without any regard for municipal boundaries. This is especially the case for so-called linear structures, such as pipelines and power transmission lines. In principle, the competent tax authority is the tax authority of the municipality where the structure is located. However, when a structure is located in several municipalities, the value of the part of the structure located in a given municipality is determined in proportion to the length of the section of the structure located in that municipality.[6]

This solution is only seemingly simple. The length of a structure is a rather imprecise way to allocate revenues from property tax. On objects such as power grids or pipelines, there are various devices which can be treated as parts of the structure.[7] Their value, however, will not be taxed in the municipality where they are located, but will be "divided" among the municipalities in the territory of which the structure is located, in the proportion corresponding to the length of the structure.

The division of the value of structures between municipalities is difficult from a practical point of view. In the case of structures that form technical networks (electricity, gas, etc.), it is difficult to indicate the boundaries of the structure in question. In practice, such networks are often built gradually. Gradually, individual stages of network construction are "recorded" in the taxpayer's documentation as separate fixed assets for the purpose of their depreciation. Since it is the value of a fixed asset that is the tax base in the case of depreciated structures, in practice, it is this value, and not the value of the structure, that will be subject to "division" between municipalities.

There are also procedural problems. Each of the tax authorities will conduct separate tax proceedings when it disagrees with the taxpayer's position on the taxation of a structure. It may therefore calculate the length of a section of a structure in its municipality differently. If a structure is not depreciated, the tax base will be its market value. Each municipality will conduct separate tax proceedings during which different experts may arrive at different valuations of structures. Unfortunately, Polish law does not allow these tax proceedings to be conducted jointly.

The distribution of tax revenue for structures does not take into account the costs incurred by neighbouring municipalities for the operation of these structures. In the case of complex industrial facilities, it is necessary to provide access roads, public transport for employees (which is not free of charge, of course, but the municipality has to bear the costs of organising it), schools for employees' children, etc. These

[4] Article 6 F.T.A., Article 6a(4a) and (5) A.T.A., Article 1c, Article 6(6) and (7) L.T.C.A.

[5] Article 1c, Article 6(6) and (7) L.T.C.A.

[6] Article 4(9) L.T.C.A.

[7] Usually, these are technical devices and should not be taxed, but practice varies.

costs are sometimes borne by municipalities other than those in which the plant is located.

Of course, a tax is not a payment for a municipality's services, but this does not exclude the feeling of injustice in some cases. This is very evident in the case of large coal-fired power facilities. A lignite mine covers a considerable area of land and increases the revenue from its taxation; additionally, it means considerable revenue from the exploitation fee. However, the neighbouring municipality does not receive such income, and it may also have a problem providing drinking water to its inhabitants.[8] Of course, the entrepreneur may be obliged to remove such negative effects of its activity, which does not change the fact that some communes derive tax benefits which compensate for their inconvenience, while others are deprived of such tax benefits.

There are situations where a large energy investment is located in a small municipality, resulting in relatively high tax revenue for that municipality. An example of such a municipality existed until the end of 2016. Dobrzeń Wielki (currently approx. 10,000 inhabitants), where a large power plant, "Opole," was located, was, incidentally, situated right on the border of the city of Opole (currently approx. 120,000 inhabitants). The power plant paid PLN 25,000,000 annually to the municipality in property tax.[9] As of 1 January 2017, part of the municipality (on which the power plant was located) was annexed to the neighbouring city of Opole. This meant serious financial problems for the municipality of Dobrzeń Wielki, and an increase in revenue for Opole. Of course, the change of boundaries had its justification, as the power plant was closely linked to Opole, where many of its employees probably lived.

However, this case illustrates a problem with coal-fired power generation facilities. The production of energy from coal tends to be concentrated in large power plants, just as the extraction of energy resources takes place within large mines. This results in tax revenues being concentrated at one point rather than evenly distributed over a larger area. Unfortunately, Polish law does not ensure the participation of neighbouring municipalities in the tax revenue of the municipality (where a coal-fired power plant is located, for example).

The energy transition would alleviate this problem. Renewable energy is much more deconcentrated. Of course, hypothetically, gigantic solar power stations could be built, but this is quite unlikely in Polish reality. Usually, renewable energy consists of a larger number of smaller power stations.

In the case of wind energy, not only is the deconcentration of investments important but also their location. The existing restrictions on the construction of wind power plants in the vicinity of buildings result in "pushing" such investments into less populated areas, i.e. usually poorer ones. Therefore, to some extent, this may result in a decrease in disproportions in the tax income of communes. In this aspect, previously poorer communes may gain income as a result of the energy transformation.

---

[8] A deep lignite mine lowers the water level over a significant area.

[9] https://nto.pl/byla-jedna-z-najbogatszych-gmin-w-polsce-teraz-nie-moze-spiac-budzetu-jak-po-pieciu-latach-od-powiekszenia-opola-wyglada-zycie/ar/c3-16055617.

Issues concerning the drawing by municipalities of revenue from income taxes are omitted here, as they are beyond the scope of this book. It is worth adding, however, that in the case of personal income tax, the criterion of income distribution among municipalities is the taxpayer's place of residence, i.e. a criterion not related to property at all. In the case of corporate income tax, shares are allocated to communes where business activity is carried out, so property plays a certain role in income distribution, although it is not subject to this tax.[10]

11.3 Allocation of Tax Revenue from Nuclear Power Plants—Closer to Economic Rationality

Specific solutions apply to the distribution of property tax revenues in the case of nuclear power plants. Although there are no such power plants in Poland, due to plans to build them that have been in existence for many years, there are quite detailed regulations for power plants of this type.

Pursuant to Article 50 of the Act of 29 June 2011 on the preparation and execution of investments in nuclear power facilities and accompanying investments,[11] a fee was introduced for the benefit of municipalities neighbouring with the municipality where the nuclear power plant is located. The amount of this fee will be 50% of the property tax paid by the taxpayers on the nuclear power plant or the part for which an occupancy permit was issued in accordance with separate provisions. The fee shall be divided into equal parts between all municipalities bordering the municipality in which the nuclear power plant or its part is located and paid to the budget accounts of each of the bordering municipalities by the 25th day of the month following the month in which the real estate tax was paid. In the event that a nuclear power plant or part thereof is located in more than one municipality, the fee shall be paid by each of these municipalities to all neighbouring municipalities.

It may not be an ideal system for distributing revenues from the taxation of large (and sometimes burdensome for the environment) facilities because it is based on a major simplification of settlements, as the size of the municipality is not taken into account. However, it is a small step towards a more even distribution of benefits from property tax on large energy-related facilities.

11.4 Offshore Wind Farms—Revenue Not for Municipalities

For many years, offshore wind farms were in a kind of 'tax haven' because no property tax could be levied on them. In fact, this was a completely hypothetical

[10] Article 9 of the Act of 13 November 2003 on revenues of local government units.

[11] Journal of Laws 2021, it. 1484.

paradise because there were no offshore wind farms in Poland. The territory of Poland includes only internal maritime waters and the territorial sea,[12] and only these areas can be part of the municipality's territory. The exclusive economic zone (where offshore wind farms are located) does not constitute the territory of Poland, despite the fact that artificial islands, structures and equipment used for, among other uses, wind for energy purposes are subject to Polish law.[13] The reason for this problem was that property tax is a local tax. Only maximum tax rates are enacted in the law. The rates applicable in a given municipality are set by the municipality itself by way of a resolution of the municipal council.[14] A resolution of the municipal council, as an act of local law, is a source of universally binding law only within the territory of the given municipality.[15] Thus, in order to determine the tax rate applicable to an offshore wind farm structure, the resolution issued by the commune council should be identified, whose area of operation includes the Polish exclusive economic zone. Since it is not the territory of Poland, it cannot be part of any commune.

When solving the problem, a solution unfavourable for municipalities (from the financial point of view) was adopted, as the property tax in the case of offshore wind farms was replaced by a concession fee, which constitutes state budget revenue (for more details, see Chap. 8. *Offshore wind farms—a special taxation regime*).

However, such a solution has a certain justification. After all, the municipality does not incur any additional costs from investment in offshore wind farms. Further, the investment does not burden the municipality's infrastructure.

11.5 Impact of Municipalities on the Taxation of Assets Used in the Energy Sector

In light of the Constitution of the Republic of Poland, theoretically, municipalities have a large influence on the amount of the tax burden on property. Pursuant to Article 168 of the Constitution, local government units have the right to determine the amount of taxes and local fees to the extent specified in the law.

The last part of this provision, which puts the decision on the extent of the municipalities' powers in the hands of parliament, is crucial. A glance at the regulations attached to L.T.C.A., A.T.A. and F.T.A. may suggest that municipalities can pursue an active tax policy that can influence energy transition. Tax regulations at the state level, in the case of property, agricultural and forestry taxes, contain only maximum tax rates, leaving municipalities otherwise full freedom in determining their amount (see Chap. 2. *Property taxation in Poland – main legal problems*). In this respect, municipalities are limited by general constitutional principles, such as the principle of equality, or EU regulations, such as the prohibition of state aid.

---

[12] Article 2(2) Marine Areas Act.

[13] Article 22 para 2 Maritime Areas Act.

[14] Article 5(1) of the Local Taxes and Charges Act.

[15] Article 87(2) of the Polish Constitution.

In addition, municipalities may introduce tax exemptions.[16] In this respect, an additional restriction is the ban on introducing exemptions that would apply to categories of taxpayers. Exemptions introduced by the municipal council may concern only the subjects of taxation. Only a law passed by the parliament may exempt certain categories of taxpayers from taxation.[17]

However, the reality is quite different. In practice, municipalities set rates at or close to the maximum level. Only the property tax rates of persons who do not conduct economic activities are sometimes lower than the maximum rates. Such fiscal policy of municipalities results from their difficult financial situation and the specificity of their income from government subsidies.

In addition to tax revenues, municipalities receive revenue in the form of subsidies from the state budget. The amount of the subsidy partly depends on the so-called tax power of the municipality. It is calculated by dividing the municipality's tax revenue by the number of inhabitants. The calculation of the subsidy is quite complicated, but the general rule is quite simple: the more money the municipality receives in the form of taxes (a municipality which achieves high tax revenues is treated as rich), the smaller the subsidy. Most importantly, in order to calculate the municipality's tax revenue per capita, the tax revenue that the municipality would achieve if it applied the maximum local tax rates and did not grant any tax exemptions is taken into account.[18] This mechanism discourages municipalities from pursuing an active tax policy. As a result, municipalities do not introduce solutions that would consist of tax incentives aimed at supporting the energy transition.

[16] Article 7(3) L.T.C.A.

[17] Article 217 of the Constitution of the Republic of Poland.

[18] Article 32 of the Act of 13 November 2003 on revenues of local government units (Dz.U. of 2020, it. 23 as amended).

Chapter 12
Conclusion: Are Traditional and Renewable Sources of Energy Treated Equally by the Legislator?

Equality is a constitutional principle in Poland.[1] By nature, we expect everyone to be treated equally because we associate equality with justice. Of course, there are always questions in how equality is to be understood. Does it mean absolute equal treatment of all, or equal treatment of those who are similar, and different treatment of those who are significantly different? The natural question here is whether different rules on the taxation of facilities relating to different modes of energy production would breach the principle of equality.

Whichever way one looks at understanding the principle of equality, in view of the challenges of the energy transition, namely the move away from CO_2-based energy, absolute equality of treatment for all electricity producers will not always be something that citizens consider appropriate. For more and more of us, coal-fired power generation is a kind of activity that should be treated more harshly by the law.

It is therefore worth assessing which types of energy generation are given preferential treatment by Polish legislators. It would be difficult to apply such a comparison to infrastructure for the transmission of energy and for the transport of energy resources.

Looking at the legal regulation of property taxes presented in the previous chapters, one can get the impression that, from this point of view, all types of energy are currently treated in the same way. The land occupied for such activities is always taxed, and the same rules for the taxation of structures always apply. In the past (see Chap. 6. *Taxation of wind power plants—a case of regulatory instability),* there have been exceptions here for onshore wind farms, but now—fortunately—the Polish legislator is gradually putting an end to the absurd war against windmills.

But does equal treatment of all types of energy mean that, in fact, the tax burden on property taxes is equal? This turns out not to be the case. In fact, a number of circumstances have come together, which means that, in general, the taxation of a coal-fired power station will be lower than that of other types of power station of the same capacity.

[1] Article 32 of the Polish Constitution.

W. Morawski and A. Kałążny, *The Taxation of Energy-Sector Assets: Polish Tax Legislation on the Eve of Energy Transformation*, SpringerBriefs in Energy,
https://doi.org/10.1007/978-3-031-15673-1_12

Table 12.1 Amounts of property tax relevant for different sources of energy

Type of power plant	Onshore wind power plant	Onshore wind 2017	Offshore wind	Photovoltaic	Coal-fired
Approximate amount of annual property tax per 1 MW (PLN)	20,000–70,000	80,000–280,000	23,000	22,000	15,000

Source Kałążny and Morawski (2021, p. 14)

Above is a summary of the property tax burden of different types of power plants in Poland (Table 12.1).

The statement above requires some explanation. First, it is approximate since, especially in the case of coal-fired power plants, their construction and age are very different, and therefore the amount of tax will differ. In addition, the separation of construction and non-construction parts is based on certain simplifications and varies depending on the object. Similar facilities located in different municipalities may be taxed differently, as each authority will adopt a different method of separating the building parts. In the case of onshore wind power plants, it was necessary to separate the year 2017, when there was very often a spike in the tax burden. In the case of an offshore wind power plant, the equivalent of the property tax is the concession fee set in the lump sum of 23,000 per 1 MW of installed capacity. In the case of photovoltaic power plants (we omit here installations on buildings, which are not taxed), we rather rely on preliminary valuations by investors. The current jurisprudence of administrative courts (regarding the dispute of whether to tax the entire plant or only the built part) is rather favourable for investors. Their valuations may therefore be correct. The tax amount does not include the value of property tax paid by the mine where the coal used in the power plant is extracted.

So, how can differences in taxation be explained? The simplest explanation is simply that the assets required to produce different types of energy have different values.

However, it should also be taken into account that the value of such property for the purposes of real estate tax is assessed in a rather specific manner. The value of the real estate tax base depends on the historical value of a given object, i.e. the value of the object at the moment when it started to be subject to real estate tax. As already indicated in Chap. 2 (*Property taxation in Poland—main legal problems*), due to inflation, older objects dating from the 1990s will usually have a lower value for tax purposes. Of course, their market value and economic efficiency may also be lower now, although in the case of buildings, their efficiency sometimes decreases much less than in the case of technical equipment.

Poland has trusted coal for many years, and low-carbon power generation in Poland has developed only in the last few years, with only a few coal-fired power stations being built. As a result, in principle, older coal-fired power stations are already more lightly taxed than new 'non-coal' power stations or even newer, more environmentally friendly coal-fired power stations. In addition, the costs of building construction in Poland have been changing. The prices of building materials have risen dramatically in recent years, so new power plant facilities are also more expensive.

Determining the general level of taxation on different types of power plants (or even on the same type of power plant) in Poland is difficult because of the way the value of the tax base is determined. In Poland, two identical structures built at the same time may be taxed differently. This is because the tax base is the value by which depreciation allowances are calculated (in income taxes), which includes, inter alia, financing costs accrued up to the date on which the investment is put into service. Until recently, credit interest rates in Poland were radically higher than in western European countries. This obviously meant that the value of the tax base of a power plant built using a loan was higher than that of one built using the entrepreneur's own funds. Thus, in practice, property tax costs for onshore wind power plants varied widely, for example, and ranged from about PLN 20,000 to about PLN 70,000 per 1 MW (ignoring 2017).

In the case of hard coal and lignite power plants, it would be useful to add the burden of the tax on the mines to the above list. In the case of lignite-fired power plants, the property tax paid by mines would be comparable to that paid by power plants. Therefore, it appears that the tax burden on coal-fired power plants in the broad sense can be even higher than on renewable energy.

In the case of the tax paid by hard coal mines, this is difficult for several reasons. First, hard coal mines are not closely linked to a specific power plant, as hard coal can be transported over much greater distances. The level of taxation on hard coal mines is still the subject of disputes between tax authorities and taxpayers. Unclear rules on taxation, accompanied by unclear rules on the valuation of taxed assets, mean that differences in the level of taxation of individual hard coal mines can be significant.

Bibliography

Antonów, D. (2017). Pojęcie opłaty w polskim języku prawnym. In W. Miemiec (Ed.), *Księga jubileuszowa ku czci profesor Krystyny Sawickiej, Gromadzenie i wydatkowanie środków publicznych* (pp. 487–496).

Borszowski, P. (n.d.). Komentarz do ustawy o podatkach i opłatach lokalnych. In P. Borszowski & K. Stelmaszczyk (Eds.), Podatki i opłaty lokalne. Podatek rolny. Podatek leśny. Komentar . Wolters Kluwer, LEX. https://sip.lex.pl/#/commentary/587704804/502244.

Brzeziński, B., & Kalinowski, M. (2001). Glosa do uchwały składu 7 sędziów Naczelnego Sądu Administracyjnego 2.07.2001 r., FPS 2/01. *Przegląd Orzecznictwa Podatkowego, 1.*

Brzeziński, B. (2017). Prawo podatkowe. Zagadnienia teorii i praktyki. TNOiK Toruń.

Dowgier, R. (2018). Budynek czy budowla? Kilka uwag na tle wyroku Trybunału Konstytucyjnego z dnia 13 grudnia 2017 r, (SK 48/15). *Przegląd Podatków Lokalnych i Finansów Samorządowych, 4.*

Dowgier, R., Etel, L., Liszewski, G., & Pahl, B. (2021). In R. Dowgier, L. Etel, G. Liszewski, B. Pahl., & Podatki (Eds.), I opłat lokalnych. Komentarz (Article 2). LEX/el. Retrieved 26 May 2022 from https://sip.lex.pl/#/commentary/587865025/662465/dowgier-rafal-i-in-podatki-i-oplaty-lokalne-komentarz?keyword=pas%20ochronny%20podatek&cm=SREST.

Drofiszyn, M., & Warzel, A. (2020). Dalsze kontrowersje w sprawach opodatkowania gruntów pod liniami elektroenergetycznymi. *Przegląd Orzecznictwa Podatkowego, 1.*

Dubisz, S. (2003) Uniwersalny słownik języka polskiego. Wydawnictwo Naukowe PWN.

Etel, L. (2002). Pojęcie wyrobiska górniczego w świetle orzecznictwa Naczelnego Sądu Administracyjnego. *Państwo i Prawo, 7,*

Etel, L., & Teszner, K. (2006). Opodatkowanie podatkiem od nieruchomości urządzeń znajdujących się wewnątrz budynku stacji przekształtnikowej, *Finanse Komunalne, 5,* 22–28. https://sip.lex.pl/#/publication/151046863.

Etel, L. (n.d.) Article 1(a) Opodatkowanie budowli w budynkach, w: Podatek od nieruchomości. Komentarz. LEX. Retrieved 23 November 2018 from https://sip.lex.pl/#/commentary/587341186/138626.

Etel, L. (2022). Co wynika z uchwały NSA z 29 września 2021 r. (sygn. akt III FPS 1/21) w sprawie silosów? *Przegląd Podatków Lokalnych i Finansów Samorządowych, 1.*

Fjeldstad, O.H. (2001). Intergovernmental fiscal relations in developing countries: A review of issues, CMI Working Papers, (pp. 5–7). https://www.cmi.no/publications/file/871-intergovernmental-fiscal-relations-in-developing.pdf; Institutions of intergovernmental fiscal relations: Challenges ahead. The role of intergovernmental fiscal institutions: The case of tax sharing, https://doi.org/10.1787/9789264246966-3-en; Retrieved: 30 Jun 2022.

W. Morawski and A. Kałążny, *The Taxation of Energy-Sector Assets: Polish Tax Legislation on the Eve of Energy Transformation*, SpringerBriefs in Energy,
https://doi.org/10.1007/978-3-031-15673-1

Frużyński, A. (2012). Zarys dziejów górnictwa węgla kamiennego w Polsce. Muzeum Górnictwa Węglowego, https://depot.ceon.pl/bitstream/handle/123456789/17286/zarys_dziejow_gornictwa_wegla_kamiennego.pdf?sequence=1. Retrieved 30 June 2022.
Gomułowicz, A. (2008). In A. Gomułowicz & J. Małecki (Eds.), *Podatki i prawo podatkowe*. Lexis Nexis.
Hanusz, A. (2001). Obowiązek podatkowy w podatku od nieruchomości a wyrobiska górnicze. *Glosa, 2*, 20–28.
https://www.forum-energii.eu/public/upload/articles/files/Raport_Transformacja%20energetyczna%20Polski_2021.pdf. Retrieved 30 June 200.
https://www.national-geographic.pl/traveler/artykul/polska-dla-ciekawskich-belchatow-najwieksza-dziura-w-ziemi. Retrieved 30 Jun 2022.
https://twojeradio.fm/jeszcze-wieksze-pieniadze-z-gazoportu-w-swinoujsciu-wplyna-do-kasy-miasta.html. Retrieved 23 May 2022.
https://pl.wikipedia.org/wiki/Lista_elektrowni_w_Polsce. Retrieved 23 May 2022.
https://businessinsider.com.pl/firmy/zarzadzanie/wykonawcy-rozbudowy-terminala-lng-w-swinoujsciu-za-19-mld-zl/rjwmc0m. Retrieved 23 May 2022.
https://naftoport.pl/. Retrieved 23 May 2022.
https://www.marineinsight.com/types-of-ships/what-is-floating-storage-regasification-unit-fsru/. Retrieved 23 May 2022.
https://terminallng.gaz-system.pl/pl/terminal-lng/terminal-lng-w-swinoujsciu/. Retrieved 23 May 2022.
https://300gospodarka.pl/news/inflacja-w-polsce-na-przestrzeni-lat-wykresy-gus. Retrieved 30 Jun 2022.
https://inzynieria.com/uploaded/magazines/pdf/pe01_pierwszy_polski_terminal_lng.pdfaccessed. Retrieved 23 May 2022.
https://300gospodarka.pl/news/zielony-wodor-zamiast-gazu-w-jamale-tak-jesli-polska-dobrze-wykorzysta-swe-szanse. Retrieved 23 May 2022.
https://wysokienapiecie.pl/39431-co-polska-chce-ugrac-w-ue-przy-okazji-energetycznej-transformacji/. Retrieved: 30 June 200.
https://wysokienapiecie.pl/39431-co-polska-chce-ugrac-w-ue-przy-okazji-energetycznej-transformacji/. Retrieved 30 June 2022.
Janicki, A. (2021). Zasada rozstrzygania wątpliwości na korzyść podatnika. Analiza poglądów doktryny i orzecznictwa. Wydawnictwo UMK.
Kałążny, A. (2020b). Opodatkowanie infrastruktury podatkiem od nieruchomości. Wolters Kluwer.
Kałążny, A. (2020c). Wszystko płynie—czyli o zmienności wykładni przepisów zwalniających infrastrukturę transportową z podatku od nieruchomości. *Przegląd Podatkowy, 12*.
Kałążny, A. (2020a). Urządzenie budowlane jako budowla opodatkowana podatkiem od nieruchomości. *Przegląd Podatków Lokalnych i Finansów Samorządowych, 4*,
Kałążny, A. (2022). Nie taki diabeł straszny? komentarz do uchwały siedmiu sędziów NSA z dnia 29 września 2021 r. (sygn. akt III FSP 1/21). *Przegląd Podatków Lokalnych i Finansów Samorządowych, 4*,
Kałążny, A., & Jankowska, D. (2022). Opodatkowanie elektrowni fotowoltaicznych—im dalej w las, tym więcej drzew. *Przegląd Podatkowy, 4*.
Kielerz, A. , Beuch, W., & Marzec, R., (2018). Węgiel w energetyce zawodowej a polski mikst energetyczny. Zeszyty Naukowe Instytutu Gospodarki Surowcami Mineralnymi i Energią Polskiej Akademii Nauk, *105*, 88. https://doi.org/10.24425/124380. https://nettg.pl/news/113976/na-co-bylo-stac-przedwojennego-gornika, Retrieved 30 June 2022.
Kosikowski, C. (1999). Źródła prawa podatkowego w świetle Konstytucji. Glosa, 7,
Kowalik, P. (2012). Podział zadań i środków finansowych między różnymi szczeblami władzy—analiza porównawcza w dwóch odmiennych ustrojach państwa na przykładzie Polski i Niemiec (in:) Finanse w niestabilnym otoczeniu—dylematy i wyzwań (pod red. T. Famulska, A. Walasik), pp. 103–113.

Mariański, A. (2011). Rozstrzyganie wątpliwości na korzyść podatnika. Zasada prawa podatkowego. Wolters Kluwer Polska.

Mastalski, R. (2001). Opodatkowanie budowli w wyrobiskach górniczych. *Przegląd Podatkowy, 12*, 37–39.

Morawski, W. (Ed.) (2012). Podatek od nieruchomości w orzecznictwie sądów administracyjnych. Komentraz. Lnie interpretacyjne. Wolters Kluwer Polska, 2021

Morawski W. (2014). Zmienne koleje opodatkowania elektrofiltrów podatkiem od nieruchomości, Glosa, *1*.

Morawski, W. (2015). Wpływ zmiany definicji obiektu budowlanego na zakres przedmiotowy podatku od nieruchomości: Przypadkowa rewolucja? *Przegląd Podatkowy, 6*.

Morawski, W. (Ed.). (2009). *Ustawa o podatkach i opłatach lokalnych*. Komentarz.

Morawski, W., & Kałążny, A. (2021). Assets used to generate energy-in the context of the transformation of the Polish energy sector from coal energy to low-emission energy. *Energies, 14*(15), 4587. https://doi.org/10.3390/en14154587

Pahl, B. (2003). Morskie farmy wiatrowe zlokalizowane w wyłącznej strefie ekonomicznej a podatek od nieruchomości. *Finanse Komunalne, 3*.

Pahl, B. (2009). Opodatkowanie stacji transformatorowych. Przegląd Podatków Lokalnych i Finansów Samorządowych', 12.

Pahl, B. (2014). Glosa do wyroku WSA z dnia 16 października 2013 r., I SA/Op 327/13, LEX/el. 2014.

Pahl, B. (2019). Glosa do wyroku WSA z dnia 27 marca 2014 r., I SA/Kr 1748/13. LEX: https://sip.lex.pl/#/publication/386075647,

Popławski, M. (2015). Stacje elektroenergetyczne jako przedmiot opodatkowania podatkiem od nieruchomości. *Przegląd Podatków Lokalnych i Finansów Samorządowych, 9*.

Ruta, M. (2020). Podatek od morskich farm wiatrowych—proponowany model opodatkowania inwestycji offshore. *Przegląd Podatkowy, 6*.

https://www.lw.com.pl/pl,2,s170,charakterystyka_ogolna.html. Retrieved 30 Jun 2022.

https://www.lw.com.pl/pl,2,s338,pracownicy.html. Retrieved 30 Jun 2022.

Schwartz, H. (2012). Wyznaczenie obszaru górniczego. *Surowce i Maszyny Budowlane, 1*.

Shah, A. (2014). The reform of intergovernmental fiscal relations in developing and emerging market economies. World Bank Group, https://doi.org/10.1596/0-8213-2836-0. Retrieved 30 Jun 2022.

Wierczyński, G. (2016). Komentarz do ustawy o ogłaszaniu aktów normatywnych i niektórych innych aktów prawnych. In Redagowanie i ogłaszanie aktów normatywnych (2nd ed., electronic version, commentary to Article 5). Wolters Kluwer Polska.

www.ingramcontent.com/pod-product-compliance
Ingram Content Group UK Ltd.
Pitfield, Milton Keynes, MK11 3LW, UK
UKHW021239300926
15471UKWH00013B/765
* 9 7 8 3 0 3 1 1 5 6 7 2 4 *